LIGHT LUNCHES

◆

Reader's Digest Healthy Cooking Library

LIGHT LUNCHES

Published by The Reader's Digest Association Limited

LONDON ◆ NEW YORK ◆ SYDNEY ◆ CAPE TOWN ◆ MONTREAL

The Reader's Digest Healthy Cooking Library was edited and designed by The Reader's Digest Association Ltd, London. These recipes and illustrations have previously appeared in GREAT RECIPES FOR GOOD HEALTH, published in 1993 by Reader's Digest, UK.

First Edition

Printed in Italy

ISBN 0 276 42177 9

Consultant Editor Pat Alburey
Nutritional Consultant Editor Cynthia Robinson, BSc
Nutritional Consultant Moya de Wet, BSc, SRD

Recipes created by Pat Alburey, Valerie Barrett, Jackie Burrow, Carole Handslip, Petra Jackson, Meg Jansz, Angela Kingsbury, Danielle Nay, Louise Pickford, Jane Suthering, Judith Taylor, Hilaire Walden

CONTENTS

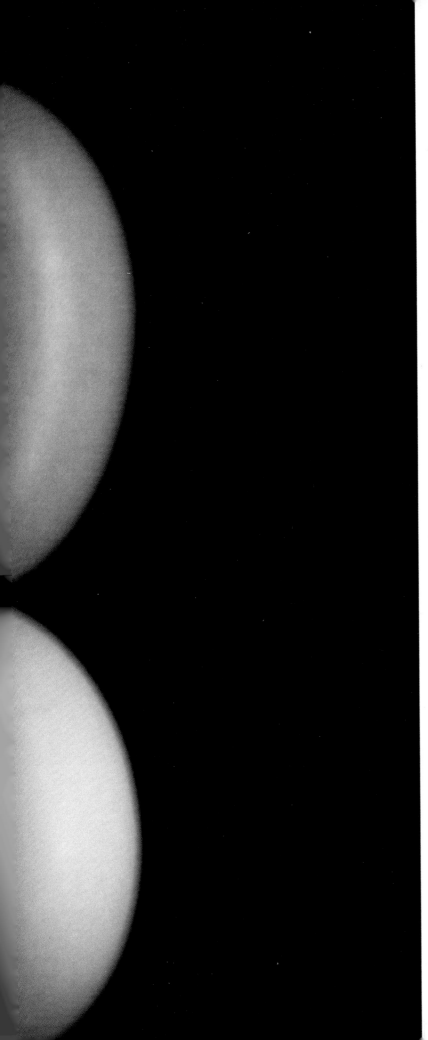

BRUNCH

*The first meal of the day
can be a dawdling
treat as you read the
newspapers, or a sociable feast
with guests. There is a recipe
here to suit any morning.*

Lean, hearty beef braised in red wine and blended with fromage frais is transformed into a light-textured spread with a rich, meaty taste.

Potted beef

ONE SERVING

CALORIES 195

TOTAL FAT 7g

SATURATED FAT 2g

CARBOHYDRATES 5g

ADDED SUGAR 0

FIBRE 0

SODIUM 90mg

SERVES 4
PREPARATION TIME: 25 minutes, plus 4 hours to cool
COOKING TIME: 1 hour 45 minutes
OVEN: Preheat to 160°C (325°F, gas mark 3)

2 teaspoons olive oil
1lb (450g) shin of beef with bone and fat removed,
cut into large cubes
¼ pint (150ml) red wine
1 clove garlic, peeled and sliced
1 level teaspoon dried marjoram
1 bay leaf
8oz (225g) low-fat fromage frais
1 level teaspoon mixed peppercorns, crushed
Fresh coriander leaves to garnish

1 Heat the oil in a frying pan and brown the meat in it on all sides over a high heat. Lift the meat out of the pan with a slotted spoon and put it in a small, ovenproof casserole.

2 Stir in the wine, garlic, marjoram and bay leaf. Cover with a tightly fitting lid and cook in the heated oven for about 1 hour 45 minutes, or until the meat is tender enough to cut with a spoon. Stir once or twice during cooking.

3 Turn the meat and liquid into a shallow dish, discarding the bay leaf. Leave to cool, then refrigerate for at least 2 hours. Lift off any fat from the top and remove and discard any membranes and gristle from the meat. Blend the meat and the cooking juices in a food processor until smooth, or mince very finely, passing it twice through a mincer.

4 Add the fromage frais and blend again for 1 minute or beat with a fork. Spoon the

mixture into four ramekin dishes, sprinkle the crushed peppercorns on top and chill in the refrigerator for 1 hour. Garnish with the coriander just before serving.

Melba toast makes a light and crisp accompaniment to the smooth potted beef.

Cheese salad in pitta bread

ONE SERVING	
CALORIES	270
TOTAL FAT	9g
SATURATED FAT	3g
CARBOHYDRATES	36g
ADDED SUGAR	0
FIBRE	1g
SODIUM	250mg

Peppery radishes and crisp carrots combine with Cheddar in a filling for pitta bread; alfalfa sprouts add a crunchy finishing touch.

SERVES 4
PREPARATION TIME: 15 minutes

1 level tablespoon Greek yoghurt
1 tablespoon white wine vinegar
½ level teaspoon dried oregano
¼ level teaspoon paprika
Freshly ground black pepper
4oz (115g) reduced-fat Cheddar cheese, cut into thin strips
1 medium carrot, peeled and coarsely grated
4 radishes, trimmed and sliced
4 pitta breads
4 cos lettuce leaves, washed and dried
2oz (60g) alfalfa sprouts

1 Combine the yoghurt and vinegar and stir in the oregano and paprika. Season this dressing with pepper, then mix in the cheese, carrot and radishes.

2 Split open the pitta breads along one side and put a lettuce leaf in each, hollow side up. Spoon the cheese mixture into the lettuce, and top evenly with the alfalfa sprouts.

You can use ricotta or well-drained cottage cheese in place of the Cheddar. For a change of flavour, use a de-seeded and chopped tomato and 1 level teaspoon chopped fresh basil instead of carrot and oregano.

Mild, mashed beans gain a hot edge from curry spices in this savoury, fibre-packed topping for toast. Fresh tomato slices moisten the dish.

Spicy beans on toast

ONE SERVING	
CALORIES	280
TOTAL FAT	8g
SATURATED FAT	1g
CARBOHYDRATES	42g
ADDED SUGAR	0
FIBRE	6g
SODIUM	205mg

SERVES 4
PREPARATION TIME: 10 minutes
COOKING TIME: 10 minutes

2 tablespoons olive oil
2 green sticks celery, trimmed and finely chopped
1 medium red onion, peeled and finely chopped
1 clove garlic, peeled and crushed
2 level teaspoons curry powder
1 level tablespoon chopped fresh savory or thyme
14oz (400g) cooked borlotti, cannellini or haricot beans, drained and mashed
4 slices crusty bread
Tomato slices and coriander leaves to garnish

1 Heat the oil in a frying pan and cook the celery and onion in it over a moderate heat for 6-8 minutes, stirring frequently, until softened but not browned.

2 Stir in the garlic, curry powder and savory or thyme, and cook for 1 minute. Mix in the beans and cook gently for 3-4 minutes, until heated all through.

3 Meanwhile, toast the bread on both sides. Spread the bean mixture on the toast and arrange the sliced tomatoes on top. Sprinkle with the coriander and serve at once.

Courgette and tomato omelette

SERVES 6
PREPARATION TIME: 10 minutes
COOKING TIME: 10 minutes

1 tablespoon olive oil
6 spring onions, trimmed and chopped
2 cloves garlic, peeled and crushed
8oz (225g) courgettes, halved lengthways and cut
into thick slices
14oz (400g) tinned tomatoes, drained and chopped
½ level teaspoon each dried basil and dried thyme
Freshly ground black pepper
3 eggs, plus 3 egg whites, size 2
2oz (60g) grated mozzarella cheese
Sprigs of fresh thyme to garnish

1 Heat the oil in a large, nonstick omelette
pan and cook the spring onions in it over a
moderate heat for about 1 minute, until
softened but not coloured. Mix in the garlic
and courgettes and cook for 3 minutes, shaking
the pan from time to time.

2 Stir the tomatoes, basil and thyme in with
the onions, and season with pepper. Cook for
about 2 minutes more, or until the courgettes
are tender and the liquid from the tomatoes
has almost evaporated.

3 Meanwhile, heat the grill and beat the
eggs and egg whites lightly with a fork. Pour
the mixture over the vegetables and stir gently
for 2 minutes, pushing the set mixture to the
centre and tilting the pan to let the unset
mixture run round the edge.

4 When the mixture is set underneath, scatter
the mozzarella over the top, and put the pan
under the hot grill for about 2 minutes, until
the omelette is set and lightly browned on top.
Cut into wedges, garnish with the thyme sprigs
and serve at once.

Crusty bread and a green or mixed salad are
good accompaniments to this dish. You can
vary the omelette filling, using leek, diced
cooked potato, red or green pepper, chopped
broccoli or chopped mixed fresh herbs. Instead
of adding cheese, scatter on 2 rashers of
unsmoked back bacon, trimmed of fat and
finely chopped.

ONE SERVING

CALORIES 115

TOTAL FAT 7g

SATURATED FAT 3g

CARBOHYDRATES 3g

ADDED SUGAR 0

FIBRE 1g

SODIUM 165mg

*Chunks of courgette and sweet tomato sparked with
spring onion, basil and thyme add texture to this
light omelette that is simple to prepare. Melted
mozzarella tops the pale egg base to give a golden
finish to a savoury brunch dish.*

Hummous savoury slices

SERVES 4
PREPARATION TIME: 15 minutes

8oz (225g) cooked chickpeas
½ level teaspoon ground cumin
1 large clove garlic, peeled and crushed
2 tablespoons olive oil
2 tablespoons lemon juice
4oz (115g) low-fat fromage frais
Freshly ground black pepper
8 slices from a wholemeal baton loaf
2 rashers unsmoked back bacon, trimmed of fat, grilled and finely chopped
4 button mushrooms, wiped and chopped
1 level tablespoon toasted sesame seeds
Sprigs of watercress to garnish

ONE SERVING

CALORIES	265
TOTAL FAT	10g
SATURATED FAT	2g
CARBOHYDRATES	31g
ADDED SUGAR	0
FIBRE	3g
SODIUM	450mg

1 Blend the chickpeas, cumin, garlic, oil, lemon juice and fromage frais in a food processor, or pass through a food mill. Season the hummous with pepper.

2 Toast the slices of bread lightly on both sides and spread them with the hummous. Top each slice with some bacon and mushrooms, and sprinkle with sesame seeds. Garnish with the watercress and serve.

Chickpea and sesame spread, served either as an appetising dip or as a side dish in the Middle East, is given an English-breakfast flavour here with a sprinkling of bacon and mushrooms.

Double haddock kedgeree

ONE SERVING

CALORIES	260
TOTAL FAT	7g
SATURATED FAT	2g
CARBOHYDRATES	25g
ADDED SUGAR	0
FIBRE	0
SODIUM	625mg

SERVES 4
PREPARATION TIME: 15 minutes
COOKING TIME: 20 minutes

4oz (115g) long grain and wild rice mixture
8oz (225g) fresh haddock
8oz (225g) smoked haddock

2 eggs, size 2, hard-boiled and shelled
5 level tablespoons Greek yoghurt
1 level tablespoon chopped fresh parsley
Freshly ground black pepper

1 Cook the rice and set it to one side.

2 Meanwhile, put the fresh and the smoked haddock into separate pans, cover with water and bring to the boil. Cover and simmer for about 10 minutes, until the flesh flakes easily. Drain the haddock, remove the skin and bones and break the flesh into large flakes.

3 Cut the hard-boiled eggs in half. Take out and sieve the yolks, then set aside. Roughly chop up the egg whites.

4 Mix the rice, fish, egg whites, yoghurt and parsley in a large saucepan, and season with pepper. Heat gently for 2-3 minutes, stirring until hot all through. Turn the kedgeree onto a warmed serving dish and scatter the egg yolk over the top.

Instead of adding parsley, you can add ½ level teaspoon of curry powder to the kedgeree just before heating it through.

The Victorians adopted this Indian dish for their gargantuan breakfasts, whose descendant, brunch, is now the ideal time to eat kedgeree.

Kidneys in tomatoes

ONE SERVING

CALORIES 170

TOTAL FAT 7g

SATURATED FAT 2g

CARBOHYDRATES 8g

ADDED SUGAR 0

FIBRE 2g

SODIUM 245mg

Beef tomatoes serve as tender cases for a hearty filling of kidneys and mushrooms, whose juices are the basis of a rich sauce.

SERVES 6
PREPARATION TIME: 35 minutes
COOKING TIME: 15 minutes
OVEN: Preheat to 190°C (375°F, gas mark 5)

6 beef tomatoes, each about 8oz (225g)
1½ tablespoons olive oil
12 lambs' kidneys, skinned, halved and cored
12oz (340g) mushrooms, wiped and chopped
Freshly ground black pepper
1½ level tablespoons wholemeal flour
1 level teaspoon fresh rosemary leaves

1 Slice the top off the tomatoes and set aside. Use a serrated grapefruit spoon or a teaspoon to scoop out the core and seeds without piercing the flesh. Put the tomato cases upside-down on kitchen paper to drain well.

2 Heat the oil in a saucepan, stir in the kidneys and mushrooms, and season with pepper. Cover and cook gently for 10 minutes, stirring occasionally.

3 Lift out the kidneys and mushrooms with a slotted spoon and set aside. Whisk the flour into the liquid left in the pan and bring to the boil, stirring continuously until thickened. Mix in the kidneys and mushrooms. Spoon 2 kidney halves and some sauce into each tomato and push 2 or 3 rosemary leaves into each one.

4 Put the tomatoes in a baking dish, place the reserved tops on them and cook in the heated oven for about 15 minutes, or until they soften.

Smoked mackerel pâté

SERVES 4
PREPARATION TIME: 15 minutes, plus 2 hours to chill

8oz (225g) smoked mackerel fillets, skinned, flaked and any bones removed

4oz (115g) low-fat fromage frais
Finely grated rind of ½ lime
1 teaspoon lime juice
4 level tablespoons chopped watercress leaves
Freshly ground black pepper
Lime twists to garnish

TIP
To make a lime twist, take a thin slice of lime and make a cut from the centre to the edge. Twist the points of the cut in opposite directions and stand the slice on the pâté.

The strong peppery flavour of watercress offsets the richness of the mackerel in this pâté, which is blended to a soft creaminess with fromage frais.

1 Using a fork, crush the mackerel in a mixing bowl, then beat in the fromage frais well.

2 Stir in the lime rind and juice, and the watercress. Season with pepper and mix well.

3 Spoon the mixture into a serving dish, cover and refrigerate for at least 2 hours and up to 4 hours. Serve the pâté chilled, garnished with twists of lime. Offer crisp rounds of hot toast with it, or serve it with warmed wholemeal or white rolls

You can use 1 level tablespoon of soft green peppercorns in place of the chopped watercress and ground pepper.

15

Scrambled eggs Benedict

SERVES 4
PREPARATION TIME: 10 minutes
COOKING TIME: 10 minutes

1oz (30g) polyunsaturated margarine
½ oz (15g) plain flour
8fl oz (225ml) chicken stock
1 tablespoon lemon juice
Freshly ground black pepper
4 eggs, size 2
2 tablespoons skimmed milk
4 very thin slices boiled ham, about 4oz (115g)
together, fat removed
4 slices wholemeal bread
2 level tablespoons chopped fresh parsley
Fresh parsley sprigs to garnish

TIP
Take the scrambled eggs off the heat as soon as they become creamy. They will continue to cook in their own heat while you serve out the ham and, if overcooked, will become rubbery.

1 Heat half the margarine in a small saucepan, mix in the flour and cook gently for 1 minute, stirring. Gradually stir in the stock and lemon juice, then season with pepper and bring to the boil over a moderate heat, stirring all the time. Lower the heat and simmer for 2-3 minutes, stirring frequently until the sauce has thickened. Cover and set aside.

2 Whisk the eggs lightly with the milk and season with pepper. Put the remaining margarine in a small nonstick saucepan and set to melt over a low heat.

3 Meanwhile, heat the grill to medium, wrap the ham in foil and place it in the grill pan under the rack. Arrange the bread on the rack and put it under the grill, toasting it lightly on both sides.

4 While the bread is toasting, pour the egg mixture into the melted margarine and stir continuously over a low heat for about 3 minutes, until it is thickened to a smooth, creamy consistency.

5 Put the toast on warmed plates, lay a slice of ham on top and spoon a share of the egg onto each serving. Pour on the sauce, sprinkle with the parsley and serve at once with a sprig of fresh parsley garnishing each serving.

Softly set eggs are piled on crisp toast and wafer-thin ham and topped with a smooth chicken sauce, in a hearty dish for a late Sunday breakfast. For those who like their eggs in a lighter morning dish, French toast offers puffy and crisp triangles of bread that have absorbed the orange-flavoured egg.

Orange French toast

ONE SERVING

CALORIES 135

TOTAL FAT 7g

SATURATED FAT 1g

CARBOHYDRATES 13g

ADDED SUGAR 0

FIBRE 0

SODIUM 175mg

SERVES 4
PREPARATION TIME: 5 minutes
COOKING TIME: 5 minutes

2 eggs, size 2
6fl oz (175ml) skimmed milk
1 level tablespoon finely grated orange rind
4 slices 3-day-old wholemeal bread, ¼ in (6mm)
thick, cut in half and crusts removed
1 tablespoon corn oil

1 Whisk the eggs, milk and orange rind together and pour into a wide, flat dish. Lay the bread in it in one layer and after 10-15 seconds, turn over with a palette knife. Leave for 2-3 minutes to soak up all the mixture.

2 Heat the oil in a large nonstick frying pan and cook the bread over a moderately high heat for 2-3 minutes on each side, until lightly browned. Serve at once while hot and crisp.

Pork and pheasant pie

SERVES 8
PREPARATION TIME: 1 hour, plus 3 hours to cool
and overnight refrigeration
COOKING TIME: 1 hour 45 minutes
OVEN: Preheat to 190°C (375°F, gas mark 5)

TIP
To put the stock in the pie, pour it through a small funnel inserted into the hole in the pie lid. First make sure that the way in is clear by putting a teaspoon handle through the hole at an angle and sweeping it all round gently to loosen any meat sealed to the pie lid.

For the pastry:
12oz (340g) plain flour
4oz (115g) polyunsaturated margarine
4fl oz (115ml) water
1 egg, size 3, beaten

For the filling:
1½ lb (680g) pork without fat or bone, minced
1 small cooking apple, peeled, cored and grated
1½ oz (45g) fresh wholemeal breadcrumbs
2 level teaspoons dried rubbed sage
2 level teaspoons green peppercorns in brine, rinsed and drained
1lb (450g) uncooked pheasant meat (from 2 small birds) without skin or bone, cut into small cubes
½ pint (285ml) chicken stock
2 level teaspoons gelatine

1 Sift the flour into a bowl and make a well in the centre. Put the margarine and water to heat slowly in a small saucepan so that the margarine melts before the water boils.

2 Meanwhile, mix the pork in a bowl with the apple, breadcrumbs, sage and peppercorns.

3 When the water is just boiling, pour the margarine and water mixture into the flour and mix to form a dough. Knead on a lightly floured surface until smooth and pliable. Cut off a quarter of the dough and cover with an upturned pudding basin. Quickly press the rest of the pastry over the base and up the sides of a loose-bottomed tin 7in (18cm) in diameter with a spring-clip side 3¼ in (80mm) deep.

4 Spoon a third of the pork mixture over the pastry base, cover with half the pheasant meat and press down well. Repeat these two layers, then finish with the remainder of the pork mixture, mounding it slightly in the centre.

5 Roll out the remaining pastry to a round large enough to cover the pie. Moisten the edges of the pastry case with a little beaten egg, lay on the pastry top and press the edges together. Trim and crimp the edges.

6 Roll out the pastry trimmings and cut into leaves. Brush the top of the pie with beaten egg and make a hole in the centre for steam to escape during cooking. Arrange the leaves on top and brush with egg; cover the remaining egg and put it in the refrigerator until later.

7 Place the pie tin on a baking tray and bake for 1 hour 30 minutes in the heated oven. Halfway through cooking, cover loosely with foil so that the top does not brown too much.

8 Gently remove the side of the tin and brush the side of the pie with the reserved egg. Return the pie to the oven and bake for about 15 minutes more to brown and crisp the side.

9 Take the pie out of the oven, leave it on the tin base and baking tray and cover it with flyproof gauze or a meat cage. Leave it in a cool place for about 3 hours, then gently replace the cleaned side of the tin.

10 Pour 3 tablespoons of the stock into a saucepan. Sprinkle in the gelatine and leave it for 5 minutes to swell. Stir over a low heat until the gelatine has dissolved, then mix in the remaining stock and leave for 30 minutes, or until the mixture starts to thicken.

11 Carefully pour a little stock at a time through the hole in the top of pie. Let the stock settle and find its level before adding more. Fill until the stock starts to overflow. Refrigerate the pie overnight so that it sets completely.

If you wish, you can stir 1 level teaspoon of finely chopped fresh parsley into the stock just before pouring it into the pie.

Lean pork, flavoured with apple and sage and enriched with layers of pheasant, fills a grand raised pie that turns a brunch for guests into a sumptuous occasion. Serve it out of doors with a leafy salad, a spoonful of relish and fruit to follow – and the heartiest appetite will be content until evening.

Cheese rarebit

SERVES 4
PREPARATION TIME: 15 minutes
COOKING TIME: 10 minutes

3fl oz (85ml) skimmed milk
½ teaspoon Worcestershire sauce
1 level teaspoon English mustard powder
5oz (150g) grated reduced-fat Cheddar cheese
4 thick slices wholemeal bread
½ level teaspoon paprika
Sprigs of watercress and red onion rings to garnish

ONE SERVING	
CALORIES	210
TOTAL FAT	7g
SATURATED FAT	4g
CARBOHYDRATES	21g
ADDED SUGAR	0
FIBRE	3g
SODIUM	505mg

1 Stir the milk, Worcestershire sauce, mustard powder and cheese in a small, heavy-based saucepan over a low heat until the cheese has melted and the mixture is smooth. Remove from the heat and leave to cool and thicken for 10 minutes, stirring from time to time.

2 Toast the bread under a moderately hot grill on one side only. Spread the cheese mixture on the untoasted sides and sprinkle with paprika.

3 Turn the grill up to high and cook until the topping is golden brown and bubbly. Lift the slices onto individual plates, garnish with the watercress and onion, and serve immediately.

The most traditional of British ingredients – English mustard, Worcestershire sauce and Cheddar cheese – melt and sizzle over toast to create this simple snack.

Fish rarebit

ONE SERVING

CALORIES 280

TOTAL FAT 6g

SATURATED FAT 3g

CARBOHYDRATES 24g

ADDED SUGAR 0

FIBRE 3g

SODIUM 585mg

SERVES 4
PREPARATION TIME: 15 minutes
COOKING TIME: 25 minutes
OVEN: Preheat to 190°C (375°F, gas mark 5)

2 level tablespoons plain flour
¾ level teaspoon English mustard powder
¼ pint (150ml) stout or bitter beer

Freshly ground black pepper
4oz (115g) grated reduced-fat Cheddar cheese
1lb (450g) haddock, cod or other white fish
without skin or bone, cut into cubes
4 thick slices wholemeal bread
1 level tablespoon snipped fresh chives or chopped
fresh parsley

Any white fish is suitable for this variation of Welsh rarebit; baking the fish in stout produces a distinctive malty flavour and a rich sauce.

1 Mix the flour and mustard to a smooth paste in a bowl with a little of the stout or beer. Season with pepper and gradually mix in the rest of the stout or beer. Stir in the cheese and fish, and turn into an ovenproof dish.

2 Cover the dish and bake in the heated oven for 15 minutes, then uncover and bake for

about 10 minutes more, until the sauce is bubbling and the fish is cooked enough to flake easily when tested with a fork.

3 Toast the bread on both sides and lay it on individual plates. Spoon the rarebit onto the toast, sprinkle with the chives or parsley, and serve immediately.

Pork and bean tacos

MAKES 12
PREPARATION TIME: 1 hour 10 minutes
COOKING TIME: 40 minutes
OVEN: Preheat to 160°C (325°F, gas mark 3)

ONE FILLED TACO	
CALORIES 205	
TOTAL FAT 9g	
SATURATED FAT 2g	
CARBOHYDRATES 22g	
ADDED SUGAR 0	
FIBRE 2g	
SODIUM 40mg	

TIP
To fill and fold a taco, put a spoonful of filling in the centre, turn the bottom third of the taco over it, then turn in the two sides to overlap in the centre and make an open envelope shape.

For the filling:
4oz (115g) dried mixed beans, soaked in cold water overnight
1 small hock or knuckle end of pork, about 1½ lb (680g) including the bone, skin and fat removed
1 tablespoon olive oil
1 small onion, peeled and chopped
1 large clove garlic, peeled and crushed
½ medium green pepper, de-seeded and chopped
1 level teaspoon chilli powder
½ level teaspoon each ground coriander and ground cumin
14oz (400g) tinned tomatoes
4oz (115g) cos lettuce, washed and finely shredded
3 spring onions, trimmed and cut into fine strips

For the tacos:
8oz (225g) unbleached plain flour
¼ pint (150ml) boiling water
1 teaspoon sesame oil

1 Cook the beans, putting the pork in to cook with them.

2 Meanwhile, make the tacos. Sift the flour into a mixing bowl and make a well in the centre. Pour in the boiling water and mix to a firm dough, then knead on a lightly floured surface until smooth. Cover and leave to rest for 15 minutes.

3 Knead the dough again and roll it out with a rolling pin on a floured surface until ¼ in (6mm) thick. Stamp out circles with a plain cutter 2½ in (65mm) in diameter, then knead and roll the trimmings and stamp out more circles. There should be 12 in all.

4 Brush 6 circles with sesame oil and lay the remaining 6 circles on top of them. Roll out the sandwiched pairs on a floured surface until the circles are 6in (15cm) in diameter.

5 Cook the tacos one sandwiched pair at a time in an ungreased heavy-based frying pan over a moderate heat. When the sandwich starts to puff with air bubbles, after about 1 minute, turn it over and cook for 1 minute more, or until the underside is freckled with small brown spots. Lift out the tacos and carefully peel apart the two layers. Lay the tacos in an ovenproof dish, put on the lid and set aside. Cook the other pairs in the same way.

6 When the beans and pork are cooked, remove the pan from the heat and drain. Take the meat off the bone and cut it into shreds.

7 Heat the olive oil in a heavy-based saucepan and fry the onion in it for 3 minutes. Mix in the garlic and pepper, and cook for 2 minutes, then stir in the chilli powder, coriander, cumin, tomatoes, beans and pork. Bring to the boil, cover and simmer gently for 30 minutes, then turn into a warmed serving dish.

8 Fifteen minutes before the beans are ready, put the tacos to warm through in the heated oven. Pile the hot tacos on a warmed serving plate to take to the table. Serve the beans, lettuce and spring onions in separate bowls for folding in the tacos at the table.

You can prepare the tacos and bean filling the day before, if more convenient. Store the tacos in a polythene bag in the refrigerator and allow 5 minutes longer for reheating in the oven. Store the filling, once cooled, in a covered dish in the refrigerator and, before serving, bring it to the boil quickly in a saucepan, then simmer it for 10 minutes.

A stack of fresh, warm Mexican pancakes, spicy beans and pork, crisp shreds of lettuce and strips of hot spring onions make a colourful contribution to a spread for entertaining guests or family at brunch. The diners will enjoy the novelty of filling and folding their tacos at the table.

Marinated tuna and tomato sandwiches

ONE SERVING

CALORIES 265

TOTAL FAT 10g

SATURATED FAT 2g

CARBOHYDRATES 29g

ADDED SUGAR 0

FIBRE 2g

SODIUM 455mg

*Superbly soggy by
design, these unusual
and filling sandwiches
hold tuna salad in
garlic-flavoured bread
that has soaked up an
oil and vinegar dressing.*

*MAKES 4 sandwiches
PREPARATION TIME: 15 minutes,
plus 45 minutes to stand*

*8 slices bread, ¼ in (6mm) thick, from
a 1lb (450g) loaf
4 teaspoons olive oil
2 cloves garlic, peeled, halved and lightly crushed
8 teaspoons red wine vinegar
1 small red onion, peeled and thinly sliced
4 black olives, stoned and chopped
2 medium tomatoes, sliced
7oz (200g) tinned tuna in oil, drained and flaked
4 level tablespoons chopped fresh basil*

1 Cut pieces of waxed or greaseproof paper for
wrapping up the sandwiches, and lay 2 slices of
bread on each. Trickle ½ teaspoon of oil evenly
over each slice, then rub each pair of slices with
half a garlic clove. Sprinkle 1 teaspoon of
vinegar on each slice of bread.

2 Spoon equal amounts of the onion, olives,
tomatoes, tuna and basil onto one slice of each
sandwich and top with the remaining slice,
putting it oil-side down.

3 Wrap up the sandwiches securely and leave
them to stand at room temperature for
45 minutes before eating so the bread absorbs
the juices. If you are preparing a packed
lunch, keep the wrapped sandwiches in the
refrigerator until it is time to pack them, then
put them in a plastic box.

A colourful selection of vegetables smothers toasted french bread and glistens with melted Gruyère for satisfying late morning munching.

Hot vegetable baguettes

ONE SERVING	
CALORIES 435	
TOTAL FAT 13g	
SATURATED FAT 6g	
CARBOHYDRATES 64g	
ADDED SUGAR 0	
FIBRE 5g	
SODIUM 740mg	

SERVES 4
PREPARATION TIME: 15 minutes
COOKING TIME: 20 minutes

1 tablespoon olive oil
1 medium red onion, peeled and thinly sliced
1 medium red pepper, de-seeded and cut into rings
2 medium carrots, peeled and thinly sliced
2 medium courgettes, trimmed and thinly sliced
8oz (225g) tomatoes, skinned, de-seeded and chopped
1 level teaspoon chopped fresh oregano
Freshly ground black pepper
2 baguettes, each about 12in (30cm) and 7oz (200g)
3oz (85g) grated Gruyère cheese

1 Heat the oil in a frying pan, and cook the onion in it, covered, for about 5 minutes, until it is transparent. Mix in the red pepper, carrots and courgettes, then cover and cook for another 8-10 minutes.

2 Stir in the tomatoes and oregano and season with black pepper. Cook, uncovered, for 2 minutes more to evaporate the liquid.

3 Cut the baguettes in half lengthways and toast them lightly on both sides under a moderately hot grill.

4 Spread the vegetables over the baguettes and sprinkle with the Gruyère. Grill for 1 minute, or until the cheese has melted. Serve the baguettes at once while hot and crisp.

For a picnic, cool the baguettes, then wrap individually in waxed or greaseproof paper.

SOUPS AND STARTERS

Hearty winter broths and classic summer soups can please both eye and palate, but the choice of dishes to start a meal does not end there. Try a vivid medley of succulent grilled and dressed peppers, brochettes of tender scallops, little salmon and asparagus pots or a creamy confection of mushrooms held in feather-light pastry flowers. Such appetising, low-calorie treats are the promising preludes to healthy meals.

Apple and carrot soup

SERVES 6
PREPARATION TIME: 20 minutes
COOKING TIME: 35 minutes

1 tablespoon olive oil
1 medium red onion, peeled and chopped
1 stick celery, trimmed and chopped
1lb (450g) carrots, peeled and sliced
8oz (225g) cooking apples, peeled, cored and chopped
1¾ pints (1 litre) chicken stock
½ level teaspoon dried sage
1 bay leaf
Freshly ground black pepper
12 thin slices of red-skinned apple, soaked in lemon juice, to garnish

ONE SERVING

CALORIES 80

TOTAL FAT 3g

SATURATED FAT 0

CARBOHYDRATES 14g

ADDED SUGAR 0

FIBRE 3g

SODIUM 25mg

1 Heat the oil in a large saucepan, and cook the onion, celery, carrots and apple in it over a moderate heat, uncovered, for about 5 minutes, until the onion begins to soften.

2 Stir in the stock, sage and bay leaf, and season with pepper. Bring to the boil, cover and simmer for about 25 minutes, or until the carrots become tender. Discard the bay leaf.

3 Pass the soup through a food mill, or let it cool for 5 minutes and then blend it in a food processor for 1 minute. Return the soup to the pan and reheat, stirring continuously. Serve in warmed soup bowls, with each serving garnished with 2 apple slices.

Apple is an unusual ingredient in a soup, but its smooth, acid pulp thickens and sharpens this delicate combination of carrot and chicken.

Baking the aubergines concentrates the flavour they bring to this partnership with red peppers in a full-bodied and vivid soup. A hint of vinegar and ginger adds the crucial spark.

TIP
Be sure to bake the aubergines until they are very tender. This rids them of their bitterness and also gives them a distinctive, strong smoky flavour.

ONE SERVING

CALORIES 105

TOTAL FAT 5g

SATURATED FAT 1g

CARBOHYDRATES 13g

ADDED SUGAR 0

FIBRE 5g

SODIUM 70mg

Aubergine and sweet pepper soup

SERVES 4
PREPARATION TIME: 20 minutes
COOKING TIME: 45 minutes
OVEN: Preheat to 180°C (350°F, gas mark 4)

3 small aubergines, about 1 1/2 lb (680g) together
1 tablespoon olive oil
1 large onion, peeled and chopped
2 cloves garlic, peeled and chopped
1 level teaspoon peeled and grated root ginger, or 1/8 level teaspoon ground ginger
2 medium red peppers, de-seeded, halved and sliced
1/8 level teaspoon salt
1 1/4 pints (725ml) chicken stock
4 teaspoons red wine vinegar
4 rounded teaspoons low-fat natural yoghurt
Snipped chives to garnish

1 Prick each aubergine with a fork in several places. Lay the aubergines on a baking tray and cook in the heated oven for 40 minutes, or until they are tender.

2 Meanwhile, heat the oil in a saucepan for 1 minute, and gently cook the onion, garlic and ginger in it, uncovered, for 10 minutes, or until the onion softens. Mix in the peppers and the salt. Cover, and cook for a further 10 minutes.

3 Pour in the stock and simmer, uncovered, for 20 minutes, or until the peppers are very soft. Remove from the heat and drain, reserving the liquid and vegetables in separate bowls.

4 Halve the aubergines, scoop out the flesh and chop it. Blend the aubergine flesh, drained vegetables and 7fl oz (200ml) of the reserved liquid in a food processor for 1 minute, or pass through a food mill.

5 Pour into a saucepan and add the rest of the reserved liquid and the vinegar. Stir over a moderate heat for 5 minutes. Serve in warmed bowls and garnish with a spoonful of the yoghurt sprinkled with chives.

A fresh, minty prickle infuses this cream of chicken soup, which is light yet crammed with tender shreds of chicken. Lemon rind and juice highlight the refreshing flavour.

Minted chicken soup

SERVES 4
PREPARATION TIME: 10 minutes
COOKING TIME: 15 minutes

1oz (30g) polyunsaturated margarine
2 level tablespoons plain flour
1½ pints (850ml) chicken stock
½ pint (150ml) skimmed milk
½ level teaspoon finely grated lemon rind
1 tablespoon lemon juice
12oz (340g) uncooked chicken breast without skin or bone, cut into fine strips
2 level tablespoons chopped fresh mint leaves
Whole mint leaves to garnish

1 Melt the margarine in a saucepan over a low heat. Stir in the flour and cook for 3 minutes, stirring continuously.

2 Gradually mix in about a third of the chicken stock, then add the rest and the milk. Add the lemon rind and juice and bring to the boil, stirring continuously.

3 Stir in the chicken, bring back to the boil, then simmer for 5-6 minutes, until the chicken is cooked through. Scatter in the chopped mint and serve in warmed soup plates, floating the mint leaves on the soup at the last minute.

ONE SERVING

CALORIES 185

TOTAL FAT 9g

SATURATED FAT 2g

CARBOHYDRATES 6g

ADDED SUGAR 0

FIBRE 0

SODIUM 140mg

Chilled cucumber and walnut soup

ONE SERVING	
CALORIES	90
TOTAL FAT	4g
SATURATED FAT	1g
CARBOHYDRATES	8g
ADDED SUGAR	0
FIBRE	1g
SODIUM	55mg

SERVES 4
PREPARATION TIME: 10 minutes,
plus 2-5 hours to refrigerate

2 medium cucumbers, peeled, halved, de-seeded
and chopped
1 medium red onion, peeled and thinly sliced
2 tablespoons chopped fresh dill
2 tablespoons chopped fresh mint
7fl oz (200ml) skimmed milk

4oz (115g) low-fat natural yoghurt
3fl oz (85ml) chilled vegetable or chicken stock
1oz (30g) shelled walnut pieces
3 tablespoons red wine vinegar
$\frac{1}{8}$ level teaspoon cayenne pepper
Freshly ground black pepper
Sprigs of dill and paper-thin cucumber
slices to garnish
4 walnut halves, very finely chopped

Easy to make and a pleasure to eat, this refreshing summer soup is enlivened with mint and dill and enriched with yoghurt and walnuts.

1 Blend the cucumber with the onion, dill and mint in a food processor for 30 seconds, or until smooth. Add the milk, yoghurt, stock and the walnut pieces, and blend for a further 20 seconds.

2 Turn into a bowl and stir in the vinegar and cayenne. Season with black pepper, cover and refrigerate for 2-5 hours. Stir and garnish with the dill, cucumber slices and walnuts.

Minestrone

SERVES 8
PREPARATION TIME: 30 minutes
COOKING TIME: 40 minutes

ONE SERVING	
CALORIES 190	
TOTAL FAT 4g	
SATURATED FAT 1g	
CARBOHYDRATES 32g	
ADDED SUGAR 0	
FIBRE 6g	
SODIUM 60mg	

TIP
Use farfallini (tiny bows), thin spirals, short macaroni, orecchiette (little ears), or other small pasta shapes that will become very tender after 7 minutes of simmering.

1 tablespoon olive oil
2 medium onions, peeled and chopped
4 cloves garlic, peeled and chopped
2 medium carrots, peeled, cut in half lengthways and thinly sliced
1 medium potato, peeled and cut into small cubes
3 level tablespoons chopped fresh basil, or 1 level teaspoon dried basil
1 level teaspoon dried oregano
2 large bay leaves
½ lb (680g) ripe tomatoes, skinned and chopped
1¾ pints (1 litre) chicken or vegetable stock
4oz (115g) green beans, trimmed and cut into short pieces
4oz (115g) small pasta shapes
14oz (400g) cooked cannellini or flageolet beans, well drained
1 medium courgette, trimmed and diced
4 level teaspoons grated Parmesan cheese
4 level teaspoons chopped fresh parsley

1   Heat the oil in a large saucepan and cook the onions and garlic in it, uncovered, over a moderate heat for 5 minutes. Mix in the carrots, potato, basil, oregano and bay leaves, and cook for a further 5 minutes, stirring and shaking the vegetables occasionally.

2   Stir in the tomatoes, pour in the stock and bring to the boil, then reduce the heat, cover and simmer for 20 minutes. Stir in the green beans, pasta, cooked beans and courgette, and continue cooking for about 7 minutes, or until the green beans and pasta are both very tender. Discard the bay leaves.

3   Serve the minestrone in warmed soup plates and sprinkle each serving with a teaspoon of Parmesan and of parsley.

Minestrone varies from region to region in Italy, but always includes local fresh vegetables and some kind of dried beans. Pasta or rice is added according to whether the cook is from the south or the north. The result is a wholesome and filling family dish.

Smooth and thick, savoury and satisfying, this surprisingly elegant soup is made from everyday ingredients found in the store cupboard.

Split pea and potato soup

ONE SERVING	
CALORIES	235
TOTAL FAT	5g
SATURATED FAT	1g
CARBOHYDRATES	41g
ADDED SUGAR	0
FIBRE	4g
SODIUM	20mg

SERVES 4
PREPARATION TIME: 20 minutes
COOKING TIME: 55 minutes

1 tablespoon olive oil
1 medium onion, peeled and chopped
1½ pints (850ml) beef stock
4oz (115g) dried split green peas, rinsed
1lb (450g) potatoes, peeled and quartered
Freshly ground black pepper
Watercress leaves to garnish

1 Heat the oil in a large saucepan, and cook the onion in it, uncovered, over a moderate heat for about 5 minutes, until soft. Stir in the beef stock and bring to the boil.

2 Stir in the peas and potatoes, then turn down the heat, cover and simmer for about 40 minutes, or until the peas and potatoes are tender. Leave to cool for 10 minutes.

3 Purée the soup in several batches in a food processor, then reheat in the pan, stirring constantly. Season with pepper, pour into warmed plates and garnish with watercress.

Serve Italian striped bread with the pale soup.

Provençal soup

SERVES 4
PREPARATION TIME: 20 minutes
COOKING TIME: 30 minutes

1 tablespoon olive oil
4 tablespoons water
1 large onion, peeled and finely sliced
1 medium green pepper, de-seeded and chopped
1 clove garlic, peeled and chopped
1 stick celery, trimmed and finely chopped
8oz (225g) small courgettes, trimmed and thinly sliced lengthways
2 level tablespoons plain flour
1lb (450g) ripe tomatoes, skinned and chopped
1 pint (570ml) chicken or vegetable stock
1 tablespoon lemon juice
Flat-leaf parsley to garnish

ONE SERVING

CALORIES 105

TOTAL FAT 5g

SATURATED FAT 1g

CARBOHYDRATES 13g

ADDED SUGAR 0

FIBRE 3g

SODIUM 20mg

1 Heat the olive oil and water in a large saucepan and cook the onion, pepper, garlic, celery and courgettes in it over a low heat for about 5 minutes, stirring occasionally. When the water has evaporated, stir the flour into the vegetables and continue cooking for 3 minutes, stirring frequently.

2 Add the tomatoes, pour in the stock and bring to the boil, then cover and simmer for about 20 minutes. Take off the heat, stir in the lemon juice and garnish with the parsley. Serve the soup piping hot with french bread.

Olive oil, courgettes, tomatoes and garlic give the authentic character of the French country kitchen to this colourful, fresh vegetable soup.

Fresh vegetable soup

ONE SERVING	
CALORIES	125
TOTAL FAT	5g
SATURATED FAT	1g
CARBOHYDRATES	16g
ADDED SUGAR	0
FIBRE	3g
SODIUM	35mg

SERVES 4
PREPARATION TIME: 20 minutes
COOKING TIME: 30 minutes

1 tablespoon olive oil
8 button onions, peeled
3 level tablespoons plain flour
1½ pints (850ml) vegetable or chicken stock

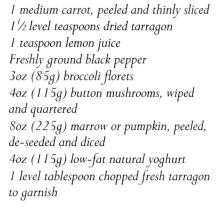

1 medium carrot, peeled and thinly sliced
1½ level teaspoons dried tarragon
1 teaspoon lemon juice
Freshly ground black pepper
3oz (85g) broccoli florets
4oz (115g) button mushrooms, wiped
and quartered
8oz (225g) marrow or pumpkin, peeled,
de-seeded and diced
4oz (115g) low-fat natural yoghurt
1 level tablespoon chopped fresh tarragon
to garnish

1 Heat the oil in a large, heavy-based saucepan and cook the onions in it over a high heat for about 5 minutes, shaking the pan from time to time to brown them all over. Lift the onions onto a plate with a slotted spoon.

2 Mix the flour into the oil left in the pan and cook over a moderate heat, stirring, for 1 minute. Gradually blend in the stock and bring to the boil, stirring continuously. Simmer for about 3 minutes until thickened.

3 Mix in the onions, carrot, tarragon and lemon juice, and season with pepper. Bring back to the boil, then lower the heat, cover and simmer for 10 minutes. Add the broccoli, mushrooms and marrow or pumpkin, cover, and cook for 5 minutes more, or until the vegetables are tender.

4 Stir in the yoghurt and reheat the soup without letting it boil or it will curdle. Pour the soup into warmed bowls, sprinkle with the fresh tarragon and serve immediately.

For a change of flavour, you can use basil instead of tarragon in the soup and as a garnish.

Broccoli, button onions and mushrooms are among the vegetables of diverse colour and texture in this chunky soup, but its distinctive character comes from the tarragon whose flavour pervades the creamy base.

Chive vichyssoise

ONE SERVING

CALORIES 155

TOTAL FAT 5g

SATURATED FAT 1g

CARBOHYDRATES 25g

ADDED SUGAR 0

FIBRE 3g

SODIUM 40mg

A generous sprinkling of chives flecks the pale creaminess of this cool, refreshing leek and potato soup and strengthens its flavour.

SERVES 4
PREPARATION TIME: 15 minutes, plus 2 hours to refrigerate
COOKING TIME: 30 minutes

1 tablespoon olive oil
6fl oz (175ml) water
1 medium onion, peeled and chopped
1 leek, trimmed, sliced and well washed
1 stick celery, trimmed and chopped
1lb (450g) potatoes, peeled and diced
1 pint (570ml) vegetable or chicken stock
7oz (200g) low-fat natural yoghurt
4 level tablespoons chopped fresh chives
1 teaspoon lemon juice
4 drops Tabasco

1 Heat the oil and 4 tablespoons of the water in a large saucepan and cook the onion, leek and celery in it, uncovered, for 8 minutes, or until the vegetables start to soften. Stir in the potatoes and cook for another 3 minutes.

2 Pour in the stock and bring to the boil, then lower the heat, cover and simmer for about 20 minutes, or until the potatoes are tender.

3 Leave the soup to cool, then blend it in a food processor until smooth. Mix the yoghurt with the remaining water and stir into the soup with the chives, lemon juice and Tabasco.

4 Cover the soup and refrigerate for at least 2 hours before serving.

Artichokes with creamed bean filling

ONE SERVING

CALORIES 160

TOTAL FAT 2g

SATURATED FAT 0

CARBOHYDRATES 27g

ADDED SUGAR 0

FIBRE 8g

SODIUM 245mg

Shallow artichoke cups make exotic containers for a smooth, thick purée of broad beans, potatoes and celeriac. The soft, filled cups have a contrasting base of crisp toast.

SERVES 4
PREPARATION TIME: 25 minutes
COOKING TIME: 15 minutes
OVEN: Preheat to 180°C (350°F, gas mark 4)

3oz (85g) potatoes, peeled and diced
3oz (85g) celeriac, peeled and diced
12oz (340g) frozen broad beans, thawed and outer skins removed
1 level tablespoon low-fat fromage frais
Freshly ground black pepper
4 slices wholemeal bread, lightly toasted
14oz (400g) tinned artichoke bottoms, well rinsed and patted dry
½ level teaspoon paprika
Red and curly endive to garnish

1 Cook the potatoes and celeriac in unsalted boiling water for about 10 minutes, or until they are tender, then drain. Cook the beans in unsalted boiling water for about 5 minutes, until tender, then drain.

2 Rub the potatoes, celeriac and beans through a sieve or vegetable mill. Stir in the fromage frais, season with pepper, and mix well to form a firm purée.

3 Cut the toast into eight triangles and arrange them in a shallow ovenproof dish. Place an artichoke bottom on each triangle of toast and spoon the bean purée onto the artichokes. Cover the dish loosely with foil and cook in the heated oven for 15 minutes.

4 Serve the filled artichokes dusted lightly with paprika and garnished with the endive.

For extra flavour, dip the edges of the toast in chopped parsley before the toppings are put on.

TIP
The slightly cupped discs of artichoke bottoms are ideal for this dish. Do not buy artichoke hearts, which are too small and have a crown of leaves attached.

Tender pieces of asparagus give a luxury flavour and flashes of colour to creamy mushroom omelettes, which make delicate starters to a meal.

Asparagus and mushroom omelettes

ONE SERVING

CALORIES 180

TOTAL FAT 14g

SATURATED FAT 3g

CARBOHYDRATES 2g

ADDED SUGAR 0

FIBRE 1g

SODIUM 130mg

SERVES 4
PREPARATION TIME: 5 minutes
COOKING TIME: 10 minutes
OVEN: Preheat to 150°C (300°F, gas mark 2)

4 teaspoons olive oil
4oz (115g) button mushrooms, wiped and thinly sliced
5 eggs, size 2
1 level tablespoon snipped chives
2 tablespoons cold water
Freshly ground black pepper
4oz (115g) cooked asparagus, chopped
1 large ripe tomato, skinned, de-seeded and chopped

1 Heat half the oil in a frying pan and toss the mushrooms in it over a high heat for about 5 minutes, until they are lightly browned and the juice has evaporated. Lift them out with a slotted spoon and drain on kitchen paper.

2 Lightly whisk the eggs, chives and water, and season with pepper.

3 Heat ½ teaspoon of the oil in a small nonstick omelette pan and stir a quarter of the asparagus and a quarter of the mushrooms in it over a moderate heat for 1 minute.

4 Turn the heat to high, pour a quarter of the egg mixture on the asparagus and mushrooms, and stir for 30 seconds with a fork, then leave to cook for 30 seconds, or until lightly set.

5 Fold the omelette in three, using a spatula. Turn it onto a hot dish, cover and put in the oven to keep hot. Make three more omelettes, then garnish them all with tomato to serve.

You can use cooked green beans, courgettes or broccoli when you cannot get asparagus.

Melon refresher

SERVES 4
PREPARATION TIME: 25 minutes,
plus 30 minutes to stand

2 small ripe Ogen or Charentais melons
6oz (175g) large ripe grapes, peeled, halved
and de-seeded
1 level teaspoon preserved ginger, very finely diced
12 melon, vine or frilled lettuce leaves, washed
and dried

1 Halve the melons crossways and de-seed them. Scoop out the flesh into a bowl without damaging the outer shell. Trim off any stalk or tail from the melon shells so that they stand like bowls. Tie the shells in a polythene bag and put them in the refrigerator.

2 Cut the melon flesh into cubes and gently mix in the grapes and ginger. Cover the bowl and leave to stand for 30 minutes for the juices to run and take in the flavour of the ginger.

3 Set the melon shells on serving plates lined with the leaves. Fill with the fruit and serve.

You can prepare the fruit the night before it is needed. Store it in a dish with a well-fitting lid and refrigerate overnight. Tie the melon shells in a polythene bag and freeze them. Take the fruit out of the refrigerator 1 hour before serving; spoon it into the frozen shells and arrange on the leaves to serve. It is quicker to use green seedless grapes and leave the skins on, but the dish is more enjoyable without skins.

TIP
Make sure you cover the melon skins or the melon cubes securely before putting them in the refrigerator or the melon flavour will penetrate other foods that are stored there.

A little ginger gives a spicy prickle to a sweet and juicy fruit salad for starting the day, whether early or on late and lazy weekends.

Pizza muffins

SERVES 4
PREPARATION TIME: 15 minutes
COOKING TIME: 5 minutes

6fl oz (175ml) tomato sauce (see p.16)
8 wholemeal muffins (see p.368)

2oz (60g) grated mature Cheddar cheese
1oz (30g) grated Parmesan cheese
4 anchovy fillets, drained and chopped
4 stoned black olives, thinly sliced
1 level tablespoon chopped fresh basil
or oregano to garnish

The soft texture of fresh muffins makes an unusual yet successful base for a pizza topping enlivened by the intense flavour of anchovies.

ONE SERVING
CALORIES 335
TOTAL FAT 13g
  SATURATED FAT 5g
CARBOHYDRATES 43g
  ADDED SUGAR 0
FIBRE 5g
SODIUM 470mg

1 Bring the tomato sauce to the boil in a small saucepan, simmer for 2 minutes and set aside.

2 Halve the muffins and lightly toast the cut sides only under a hot grill. Sprinkle the Cheddar evenly over the muffins and grill for 1-2 minutes, until the cheese melts.

3 Spread the tomato sauce over the Cheddar and sprinkle on the Parmesan. Return the muffins to the grill for 2-3 minutes, until the cheese is lightly browned and bubbling hot. Scatter the chopped anchovies and olives on top and garnish with the basil or oregano before serving.

Chicken liver croustades

ONE SERVING

CALORIES 200

TOTAL FAT 8g

SATURATED FAT 2g

CARBOHYDRATES 17g

ADDED SUGAR 0

FIBRE 2g

SODIUM 270mg

SERVES 4
PREPARATION TIME: 15 minutes
COOKING TIME: 15 minutes
OVEN: Preheat to 200°C (400°F, gas mark 6)

½ oz (15g) polyunsaturated margarine
1 level teaspoon whole-grain mustard
1 small clove garlic, peeled and crushed

4 slices wholemeal bread, ¼ in (6mm) thick,
crusts removed
8oz (225g) chicken livers, trimmed, rinsed and
patted dry, and cut into cubes
2 level teaspoons plain flour
3 tablespoons brandy or dry sherry
¼ pint (150ml) chicken stock
2 level tablespoons snipped chives
Freshly ground black pepper
Oak-leaf lettuce, thinly sliced celery and snipped
chives to garnish

1 Mix the margarine with the mustard and
garlic, and set aside.

2 Roll the bread with a rolling pin until its
thickness is about halved. Trim each slice into a
neat square and use half the mustard mixture
to spread thinly on one side of the slices.

3 Gently press the bread slices, mustard side
up, into four deep patty tins about 3½ in
(90mm) in diameter. Cook on a baking tray in
the heated oven for about 15 minutes, or until
the croustades are golden brown and crisp.

4 Meanwhile, heat the remaining mustard
mixture in a nonstick frying pan and cook the
chicken livers in it over a moderate heat,
stirring frequently, for 2-3 minutes or until
lightly browned.

5 Mix the flour into the livers and cook for
1 minute. Pour in the brandy or sherry, and
boil for 1 minute until almost evaporated.
Gradually stir in the stock and bring to the boil.
Turn down the heat and simmer, uncovered,
for 2-3 minutes until the sauce thickens.
Scatter in the chives and season with pepper.

6 Turn the croustades out of the patty tins
and set them on individual plates. Divide the
chicken liver sauce between them, garnish with
the lettuce leaves and celery and sprinkle with
the chives. Serve at once while hot.

A piquant combination of mustard and garlic
flavours the filling of chicken livers and the crisp
bread cases in which it is served. Brandy gives a hint
of sweetness to the rich sauce that coats the liver.

Duck and apple with orange dressing

SERVES 4
PREPARATION TIME: 20 minutes,
plus 20 minutes to cool
COOKING TIME: 15 minutes

Thinly pared rind of 1 orange, cut into fine strips
⅛ level teaspoon ground ginger
3 tablespoons water
1 level teaspoon cornflour
Juice of 1 large orange
1 dessert apple, washed in warm water and dried
Juice of ½ lemon
6oz (175g) cold cooked duck breast without bone or skin, cut into fine strips
1 level tablespoon blanched and chopped almonds, lightly toasted
Flat-leaf parsley sprigs to garnish

1 Simmer the orange rind with the ginger and water in a small saucepan for 10 minutes.

2 Meanwhile, mix the cornflour to a smooth cream with 2 teaspoons of the orange juice, then stir back into the rest of the juice.

3 Strain the orange and ginger mixture through a fine sieve and set aside the strips of rind. Pour the liquid back into the pan and stir in the cornflour and orange juice mixture. Bring to the boil, stirring all the time, then simmer for about 2 minutes, stirring frequently, until the mixture is clear and slightly thickened. Pour it into a bowl, cover and leave to cool.

4 Quarter and core the apple. Cut it into thin slices and immediately pour the lemon juice over them. Turn the slices in the juice until they are completely coated, so that they do not discolour.

5 When the orange dressing is cold, toss the duck in it until completely coated, then stir in the almonds. Arrange a share of the apple slices on each of four small serving plates and spoon a quarter of the duck mixture and its dressing onto each plate beside the apples. Garnish with the shreds of orange rind and the parsley sprigs. Serve at once.

ONE SERVING	
CALORIES	125
TOTAL FAT	6g
SATURATED FAT	1g
CARBOHYDRATES	6g
ADDED SUGAR	0
FIBRE	1g
SODIUM	45mg

The classic combination of duck and orange is fired by a faint trace of ginger and given a subtle crunch by toasted almonds. Apple slices make a sweet contrast.

Wild mushroom tartlets

SERVES 4
PREPARATION TIME: 15 minutes
COOKING TIME: 15 minutes
OVEN: Preheat to 180°C (350°F, gas mark 4)

ONE SERVING	
CALORIES	145
TOTAL FAT	7g
SATURATED FAT	1g
CARBOHYDRATES	16g
ADDED SUGAR	0
FIBRE	1g
SODIUM	40mg

A crisp filo pastry case like a golden flower holds spiced choice mushrooms at its heart and gets a meal off to a stylish start.

About 3oz (85g) filo pastry sheets
1½ tablespoons olive oil
2 tablespoons pale dry sherry
1 level teaspoon whole-grain or French mustard
⅛ level teaspoon cayenne pepper
3oz (85g) each fresh shiitake mushrooms and fresh oyster mushrooms, washed and halved
3oz (85g) fresh chanterelle mushrooms, washed
Mixed lettuce and endive leaves
8 level teaspoons low-fat fromage frais
Shredded purple basil or sage leaves to garnish

1 Cut the filo pastry to give twelve 4in (10cm) squares. Brush lightly on one side with oil.

2 Gently press 3 pastry squares, oiled side down, into a Yorkshire pudding tin 4in (10cm) in diameter, arranging them so that the points are evenly spaced round the rim. Form three more tartlets. Brush the inside of the tartlets lightly with the oil and bake in the heated oven for 10 minutes, until golden and crisp.

3 Meanwhile, heat the sherry gently in a frying pan, then stir in the mustard, cayenne pepper and mushrooms. Cover and cook over a low heat for 4-5 minutes, shaking the pan frequently, until the mushrooms are tender.

4 Arrange the lettuce and endive leaves on four serving plates and put a warm tartlet on each plate. Spoon in the mushrooms, top each tartlet with 2 level teaspoons of fromage frais and garnish with the basil or sage leaves. Serve at once while warm and crisp.

You can use any mixture of mushrooms to fill the tartlets. Wash wild mushrooms thoroughly and dry them with kitchen paper.

Mussel salad

ONE SERVING

CALORIES 150

TOTAL FAT 3g

SATURATED FAT 1g

CARBOHYDRATES 10g

ADDED SUGAR 0

FIBRE 2g

SODIUM 220mg

SERVES 4
PREPARATION TIME: 30 minutes,
plus 30 minutes to refrigerate
COOKING TIME: 6-8 minutes

2½ lb (1.1kg) mussels, shells well scrubbed and
scraped, beards removed
1 small onion, peeled and chopped
1 sprig each fresh thyme and fresh parsley
1 bay leaf

4fl oz (115ml) dry white wine
2 dessert apples, cored and diced
8oz (225g) celery, trimmed and thinly sliced
1 small red pepper, de-seeded and finely chopped
4 level tablespoons Greek yoghurt
2 tablespoons lemon juice
1½ level teaspoons paprika
1 level tablespoon chopped fresh mint
Freshly ground black pepper
Mixed lettuce and endive leaves, washed and dried

Mussels, which require some care in the preparation, deserve a dish that is worthy of the effort. This salad is such a dish, marrying the silky-soft mussels with crisp pieces of apple, celery and pepper, all swathed in a wine and yoghurt dressing.

TIP
To ensure the mussels are really clean rinse them in several changes of cold water after scrubbing them and removing the beards.

1 Put the mussels in a large saucepan with the onion, thyme, parsley, bay leaf and wine. Cover and cook over a high heat, shaking the pan often, for 6-8 minutes, until the shells open.

2 Line a colander with kitchen paper and place it over a bowl. Pour the mussels into the colander to drain. Discard the thyme, parsley and bay leaf, return the liquid to the pan and boil until it is reduced to about 6 tablespoons. Remove from the heat and leave to cool.

3 Remove the mussels from their shells, discarding any that are not open. Put them in a bowl with the apples, celery and red pepper.

4 Mix the yoghurt with the mussel liquid, lemon juice, paprika and mint. Season with black pepper, pour over the mussels and toss. Cover and refrigerate the salad for 30 minutes.

Arrange a bed of mixed leaves on four serving plates, spoon on the salad and serve at once.

Pheasant terrine

ONE SERVING

CALORIES 215

TOTAL FAT 8g

SATURATED FAT 2g

CARBOHYDRATES 12g

ADDED SUGAR 0

FIBRE 3g

SODIUM 325mg

SERVES 8
PREPARATION TIME: 40 minutes, plus overnight
to refrigerate
COOKING TIME: 1 hour
OVEN: Preheat to 180°C (350°F, gas mark 4)

Oven-ready pheasant, about 1½ lb (680g)
4oz (115g) mushrooms, wiped and chopped

2oz (60g) unsmoked back bacon with fat
removed, chopped
8oz (225g) chicken livers, washed and trimmed
1 red onion, peeled and chopped
2 cloves garlic, peeled and crushed
1 level teaspoon dried thyme
2 level tablespoons chopped fresh parsley
7oz (200g) tinned unsweetened chestnut purée
⅛ level teaspoon salt
Freshly ground black pepper
1lb (450g) large fresh spinach leaves, washed and
dried, thick stalks trimmed off
Fresh bay leaves, red onion rings and mixed lettuce
leaves to garnish

1 Take the pheasant meat off the bone and
remove the skin. Cut the meat into small pieces
and mince it finely or blend in a food processor
until smooth. Mix in the mushrooms, bacon,
chicken livers, onion, garlic, thyme and parsley,
and mince or blend again. Stir in the chestnut
purée and salt and season with pepper.

2 Blanch the spinach leaves for 1 minute in a
large saucepan of unsalted boiling water. Rinse
with cold water, drain and pat dry with
kitchen paper. Lay the bay leaves in a 10×5in
(25×13cm) nonstick loaf tin and line the tin
with three-quarters of the spinach leaves.

3 Spoon the pheasant mixture into the tin and
spread evenly. Arrange the remaining spinach
leaves on top. Cover the tin with a double layer
of nonstick baking paper and set it in a deep
roasting tin. Pour in enough cold water to
come halfway up the tin. Cook in the heated
oven for 1 hour, or until there is no pink in the
juices that ooze out when you push a skewer
into the middle of the terrine.

4 Lift the loaf tin onto a board and leave to
cool, then put it in the refrigerator until the
following day for the terrine to set.

Turn the terrine out and cut it into 16 slices.
Garnish it with the fresh bay, onion and
lettuce, and serve with crusty bread.

Set a celebration meal off to a grand start with this
exquisite blend of pheasant and chicken livers,
mushrooms and chestnuts, seasoned with herbs and
all meticulously wrapped in dark spinach leaves.

When the longed-for asparagus season arrives in early summer, snap up the thin, cheaper spears to use in this light, irresistible appetiser.

Salmon and asparagus ramekins

ONE SERVING	
CALORIES	95
TOTAL FAT	5g
SATURATED FAT	1g
CARBOHYDRATES	3g
ADDED SUGAR	0
FIBRE	1g
SODIUM	320mg

SERVES 4
PREPARATION TIME: 15 minutes
COOKING TIME: 30 minutes
OVEN: Preheat to 180°C (350°F, gas mark 4)

4oz (115g) thin asparagus spears, stems peeled
3 egg yolks, size 3
8fl oz (225ml) skimmed milk
⅛ level teaspoon cayenne pepper
2 level tablespoons chopped fresh dill
2oz (60g) smoked salmon, cut into thin strips

1   Cut off the asparagus tips and slice the stems thinly. Steam the tips and stems for 3-4 minutes, until just tender. Rinse with cold water to cool quickly, then drain well. Set the tips aside.

2   Whisk the egg yolks, milk, cayenne pepper and dill together. Set aside four salmon strips. Stir the rest and the asparagus stems into the egg mixture.

3   Very lightly grease four small ramekin dishes and divide the mixture between them. Stand the dishes on a baking tray and cook in the heated oven for 30 minutes, or until set.

4   Garnish the ramekins with the reserved salmon strips and asparagus tips.

You can serve the salmon and asparagus ramekins warm with hot wholemeal toast, or let them cool, then cover and refrigerate for 2-3 hours before serving.

Marinated scallop brochettes

ONE SERVING

CALORIES 110

TOTAL FAT 5g

SATURATED FAT 1g

CARBOHYDRATES 3g

ADDED SUGAR 0

FIBRE 1g

SODIUM 155mg

The exceptionally smooth yet meaty flesh of scallops benefits from a tenderising marinade, which then adds its herb and lemon fragrance to the skewers of grilled fish and vegetables.

SERVES 4
PREPARATION TIME: 15 minutes, plus at least 4 hours to marinate
COOKING TIME: 5 minutes

1 tablespoon olive oil
1 tablespoon lemon juice
1 level tablespoon chopped fresh parsley
½ level teaspoon fennel seeds, crushed
1 clove garlic, peeled and crushed
Grated rind of 1 small, gently scrubbed orange
8 fresh scallops, cleaned
1 large courgette, trimmed and cut into about 12 slices
1 medium red onion, cut into eight segments
4 metal skewers, lightly oiled

1 Mix the oil, lemon juice, parsley, fennel seeds, garlic and orange rind in a glass or china bowl and turn the scallops in the mixture until well coated. Cover and refrigerate for at least 4 hours and up to 12 hours.

2 Cover the courgette and onion with cold water in a saucepan and bring to the boil. Boil for 1 minute, then drain well.

3 Thread 2 scallops and a share of the vegetables onto each skewer. You may find it easier to thread on the scallop corals separately.

4 Lay the brochettes on a grill rack, baste with the marinade and cook under a hot grill for about 5 minutes, turning once or twice, until the white flesh of the scallops is opaque.

Serve the brochettes on warmed individual plates. You can hand round separately a small bowl of cooked brown rice mixed with chopped walnuts and watercress.

Smoked trout pâté

ONE SERVING

CALORIES 105

TOTAL FAT 3g

SATURATED FAT 1g

CARBOHYDRATES 3g

ADDED SUGAR 0

FIBRE 0

SODIUM 571mg

SERVES 4
PREPARATION TIME: 10 minutes, plus 3 hours
to chill
COOKING TIME: 10 minutes

Large fresh trout, about 10oz (275g)
8oz (225g) low-fat cottage cheese, well drained

6oz (175g) skinned and boned smoked trout,
finely flaked
1 level teaspoon grated fresh horseradish
1 tablespoon lime or lemon juice
Freshly ground black pepper
Radicchio leaves, washed and dried
Wedges of lime and dill sprigs to garnish

The delicate flesh of smoked and fresh trout is sharpened by a prudent addition of horseradish and whisked to a fluffy lightness with low-fat cottage cheese.

1 Line the grill pan with foil, lay the fresh trout on the rack and cook under a moderate heat for 4 minutes on each side, until the flesh is opaque and flakes easily. Skin and bone the fish, flake the flesh and leave until cold.

2 Use a food processor to blend the cheese, fresh and smoked trout, horseradish and lime juice until smooth. Season with pepper, put in a bowl, cover, and chill for 3 hours, or up to 12.

3 Form radicchio leaves into a cup on each serving plate and spoon in a share of the pâté. Garnish with the lime wedges and dill.

Serve the pâté with thinly sliced brown bread.

Baked tuna tomatoes

SERVES 4
PREPARATION TIME: 25 minutes
COOKING TIME: 15 minutes
OVEN: Preheat to 180°C (350°F, gas mark 4)

8 medium tomatoes
2 teaspoons lemon juice
1 tablespoon olive oil
2 tablespoons water
1 small onion, peeled and chopped
1 medium carrot, peeled and finely diced
1 level tablespoon plain flour
7fl oz (200ml) skimmed milk
7oz (200g) tinned tuna in oil, drained and flaked
1 level teaspoon capers, rinsed and drained
3 level tablespoons fine breadcrumbs
1½ level tablespoons grated Cheddar cheese
Freshly ground black pepper
Sprigs of fresh marjoram or oregano to garnish

ONE SERVING	
CALORIES	285
TOTAL FAT	17g
SATURATED FAT	4g
CARBOHYDRATES	17g
ADDED SUGAR	0
FIBRE	2g
SODIUM	355mg

1 Cut a slice off the top of each tomato and chop it finely. Scoop out the tomato seeds and cores with a teaspoon, and discard. Sprinkle the lemon juice inside the tomatoes and put them to drain upside-down on kitchen paper for 10 minutes, then pat dry.

2 Meanwhile, heat the oil and water in a frying pan and cook the onion, carrot and chopped tomato in it, covered, over a moderate heat, for about 5 minutes. Uncover and continue cooking until all the water has evaporated.

3 Stir in the flour and cook for 1 minute, then gradually mix in the milk and bring to the boil, stirring continuously. Cook for about 3 minutes, stirring, until the sauce thickens.

4 Take the pan off the heat and stir in the tuna, capers, 2 tablespoons of the breadcrumbs and half the Cheddar until thoroughly blended. Season the mixture with pepper.

5 Fill the tomato cases with the tuna mixture and stand them in a baking dish in which they will fit snugly. Sprinkle the remaining Cheddar and breadcrumbs over them and bake in the heated oven for about 15 minutes, until golden brown on top. Serve the tomatoes at once while piping hot, garnished with the sprigs of marjoram or oregano.

Versatile tuna, blended with cheese and capers, makes a high-flavour filling for tomatoes, while the cheese and breadcrumb topping adds an appetising savoury crunch to this warming dish.

Turkey and tarragon loaf

ONE SERVING	
CALORIES	140
TOTAL FAT	7g
SATURATED FAT	2g
CARBOHYDRATES	4g
ADDED SUGAR	0
FIBRE	1g
SODIUM	100mg

SERVES 8
PREPARATION TIME: 20 minutes
COOKING TIME: 40 minutes
OVEN: Preheat to 180°C (350°F, gas mark 4)

2 tablespoons olive oil
1 medium onion, peeled and finely chopped
1 large stick celery, trimmed and finely chopped

6 level tablespoons chopped fresh parsley
2oz (60g) fresh brown breadcrumbs
2 eggs, size 2, lightly beaten
1 level tablespoon chopped fresh tarragon
¼ level teaspoon freshly grated nutmeg
1lb (450g) minced uncooked turkey meat
Freshly ground black pepper
Sprigs of fresh tarragon to garnish

1 Line a loaf tin 7½ ×3¾ in (19×9.5cm) with nonstick baking paper.

2 Heat the oil in a frying pan and cook the onion and celery in it over a moderate heat for about 5 minutes, or until the onion softens.

3 Meanwhile, mix the parsley, breadcrumbs, eggs, tarragon and nutmeg with the turkey, and season with pepper. Mix in the onion and celery.

4 Spoon the mixture into the loaf tin and spread evenly. Cook in the heated oven for about 40 minutes, or until the loaf is lightly browned and there is no trace of pink in the juice that oozes out when you prick it in the centre with a skewer. Take the loaf out of the oven and leave it to stand in the tin for 15 minutes before turning it out.

5 Peel off the paper and put the loaf on a warmed serving dish. Cut it into 16 slices and garnish with the tarragon sprigs.

Serve the turkey loaf with a green salad and french bread and, if you like, a taste of apricot relish. If you are going to serve the loaf cold, leave it in the tin and when it is cool enough, put it in the refrigerator for 3-4 hours, or overnight if more convenient. Turn it out and peel off the paper to serve.

Tarragon is at its best when married to poultry, and the herb's enticing, pervasive aroma contributes much to the enjoyment of this meat loaf whether you serve it hot or cold.

POULTRY

Chicken and turkey are ever popular at the table and need never be predictable. Exploit their versatility and make simple burgers or sweet and sour apricot chicken, homely stews or exotic dishes from other continents. Poultry gives you meat as high in protein as red meat but lower in fat — if you remember to take off the skin.

American captain's chicken

SERVES 4
PREPARATION TIME: 15 minutes
COOKING TIME: 50 minutes

ONE SERVING	
CALORIES	305
TOTAL FAT	14g
SATURATED FAT	3g
CARBOHYDRATES	10g
ADDED SUGAR	0
FIBRE	3g
SODIUM	180mg

1 tablespoon olive oil
3lb (1.4kg) chicken, cut into 8 pieces, 4 breast
pieces, 2 thighs and 2 drumsticks
1 medium onion, peeled and chopped
1 medium green pepper, de-seeded and chopped
1 clove garlic, peeled and crushed
1 level tablespoon curry powder
14oz (400g) tinned chopped tomatoes
1 teaspoon lemon juice

½ level teaspoon dried thyme
Freshly ground black pepper
2 level tablespoons sultanas
1oz (30g) blanched almonds, cut into slivers

1 Heat the oil in a large frying pan and cook
the chicken joints in it over a high heat for
5 minutes, turning them to brown all over. Lift
the joints onto a plate lined with kitchen paper.

2 Gently fry the onion, green pepper, garlic
and curry powder in the pan for 5 minutes,
stirring often, until the onion softens. Stir in
the tomatoes, lemon juice and thyme, season
with pepper and simmer for 10 minutes.

3 Put the chicken pieces back in the pan and
cook, covered, for 25 minutes, or until cooked
all through and tender. Stir in the sultanas and
cook for 5 minutes more, uncovered. Arrange
the chicken on a warmed serving dish, pour the
sauce round and scatter on the almonds.

Fluffy white rice is the right base for the sweet
and spicy chicken. Give each diner a breast
piece and a leg piece and leave them to remove
the skin for themselves.

This curried chicken sweetened with sultanas is
reputed to have been the favourite dish of an
American sea captain of long ago. He is credited
with having introduced it to the southern states.

Chicken biriani

SERVES 4
PREPARATION TIME: 20 minutes
COOKING TIME: 55 minutes
OVEN: Preheat to 180°C (350°F, gas mark 4)

ONE SERVING	
CALORIES	520
TOTAL FAT	16g
SATURATED FAT	3g
CARBOHYDRATES	54g
ADDED SUGAR	0
FIBRE	2g
SODIUM	135mg

6oz (175g) long-grain rice
5 cloves garlic, peeled, 3 of them crushed
1 cinnamon stick
1 bay leaf
1 small onion, peeled and chopped
1 tablespoon lemon juice

1 level tablespoon peeled and grated root ginger,
or ½ level teaspoon ground ginger
½ level teaspoon each ground cumin, coriander
and turmeric
¼ level teaspoon each ground cinnamon, cloves,
cardamom and black pepper
8oz (225g) low-fat natural yoghurt
1lb (450g) skinned cooked chicken, cut
into cubes
2oz (60g) sultanas
2oz (60g) blanched almonds, lightly toasted

1 Cook the rice in unsalted, simmering water with the whole garlic cloves, the cinnamon stick and the bay leaf for about 12 minutes, leaving the grains still slightly hard at the centre. Rinse with cold water, drain well and discard the garlic, cinnamon and bay leaf.

2 Meanwhile, blend the onion, lemon juice, ginger, cumin, coriander, turmeric, ground cinnamon, cloves, cardamom, pepper and crushed garlic into the yoghurt. Use a food processor or beat with a wire whisk.

3 Put the chicken into a large bowl, pour on the yoghurt mixture and stir until all the meat is evenly coated.

4 Turn the chicken mixture into a shallow casserole, spoon the rice evenly on top, cover and bake in the heated oven for 35 minutes, or until the rice is completely cooked.

5 Meanwhile, cover the sultanas with cold water in a small saucepan and bring to the boil. Boil for 1 minute, then drain and keep warm.

6 When the rice is cooked, mix the rice and chicken and spoon onto a heated serving dish. Sprinkle with the sultanas and almonds.

Serve a salad of tomatoes and onion rings with the biriani. You can make the dish with turkey breast meat instead of chicken.

In India, biriani is an elaborate dish that is often served on grand occasions. The rice is an integral part, finishing its cooking on top of the meat, where it becomes fluffy and absorbs the perfumes of the spices.

Caribbean lime chicken

SERVES 4
PREPARATION TIME: 10 minutes, plus 8 hours
to marinate
COOKING TIME: 40 minutes

TIP
Never marinate food in a metal dish. The acidic ingredients (lemon or lime juice, or vinegar, for example) will react with the metal and taint the food.

Grated rind and juice of 1 lime
2 tablespoons dark rum
3 cloves garlic, peeled and crushed
2 level teaspoons peeled and grated root ginger,
or ¼ level teaspoon ground ginger
1 tablespoon hot red pepper sauce, or ½ teaspoon
Tabasco sauce
4 boneless chicken breasts, each
about 6oz (175g), skinned
1 tablespoon olive oil
1 medium onion, peeled and chopped
14oz (400g) tinned chopped tomatoes
2 tablespoons molasses or black treacle
1 cinnamon stick
2 bananas and lime wedges to garnish

1   Mix together the lime rind and juice, rum, garlic, ginger and pepper sauce or Tabasco to make the marinade.

2   Lay the chicken breasts in one layer in a glass or china dish, coat with the marinade, cover and put in the refrigerator for about 8 hours. Turn the pieces over several times.

3   Remove the chicken from the marinade and pat dry with a paper towel, reserving the marinade. Heat the oil in a frying pan and brown the chicken in it over a high heat for about 2 minutes on each side. Remove from the pan and set aside.

It is the rich rum-based marinade, sharpened by the bite of fresh lime, that gives this spicy chicken dish its distinctly Caribbean flavour.

4 Cook the onion in the pan for 5 minutes over a moderate heat, until softened. Pour the marinade into the pan and stir in the tomatoes, molasses or treacle and cinnamon stick.

5 Return the chicken to the pan and bring to the boil, then reduce the heat and simmer gently, uncovered, for 20 minutes, until the chicken is cooked right through with no pink left in the middle.

6 Lift the chicken breasts onto a heated serving dish, cover and keep hot. Boil the sauce to thicken it. Remove the cinnamon stick, pour the sauce over the chicken and garnish with sliced banana and lime wedges.

Rice and a green salad are good foils for this sweet and spicy chicken. You can marinate the chicken overnight if more convenient, turning the pieces night and morning.

ONE SERVING	
CALORIES 335	
TOTAL FAT 9g	
SATURATED FAT 2g	
CARBOHYDRATES 27g	
ADDED SUGAR 9g	
FIBRE 2g	
SODIUM 180mg	

Chicken and vegetable curry

SERVES 4
PREPARATION TIME: 25 minutes
COOKING TIME: 25 minutes

1 tablespoon vegetable oil
1 large onion, peeled and sliced
1 level tablespoon medium-hot curry powder
2 level teaspoons ground cumin
½ small cauliflower, divided into florets
1 small aubergine, trimmed and cut into cubes
1 bay leaf
¼ level teaspoon cayenne pepper
2 level tablespoons plain flour
¾ pint (425ml) chicken stock
8oz (225g) thinly sliced green cabbage
5oz (150g) fresh or frozen peas
3 cloves garlic, peeled and crushed
3 level tablespoons raisins
1lb (450g) boneless chicken breasts, skinned, beaten out thin and cut into strips
8oz (225g) low-fat natural yoghurt
2 tablespoons lemon juice
1 level tablespoon chopped fresh parsley

1 Heat the oil in a large, heavy-based saucepan and fry the onion in it gently for 5 minutes. Mix in the curry powder and cumin and cook, stirring, for 1 minute.

2 Stir in the cauliflower, aubergine, bay leaf and cayenne pepper, and cook for 1 minute. Sprinkle in the flour, then gradually mix in the stock and bring to the boil, stirring. Lower the heat, cover and simmer for 3 minutes.

3 Stir in the cabbage, peas, garlic and raisins, cover and simmer for 3 minutes. Add the chicken, bring to the boil and simmer for 5 minutes, stirring several times; discard the bay leaf. Stir in the yoghurt, lemon juice and

The combination of meat and vegetables in a rice ring makes a satisfying and balanced meal. Yoghurt gives the sauce a tartness and a creamy texture.

parsley, and heat for 1 minute without boiling or the sauce will curdle.

Spoon the curry into a ring of rice on a hot serving plate. You can garnish it with a few red pepper rings to add a touch of colour.

ONE SERVING	
CALORIES 325	
TOTAL FAT 12g	
SATURATED FAT 2g	
CARBOHYDRATES 27g	
ADDED SUGAR 0	
FIBRE 7g	
SODIUM 160mg	

Poussins with garlic

TIP

If your grill has no alternative positions for the pan, halve the poussins just before cooking and grill breast side up, turning over after 10 minutes and again after 20 minutes.

SERVES 4
PREPARATION TIME: 40 minutes, plus 2-4 hours to marinate
COOKING TIME: 30 minutes
OVEN: Preheat to 200°C (400°F, gas mark 6)

2 oven-ready poussins, each about 1¼ lb (550g)
1 tablespoon olive oil
4 fl oz (115 ml) red wine vinegar
1 bay leaf
½ level teaspoon dried thyme
½ level teaspoon dried rosemary
Finely grated rind and strained juice of 2 oranges
Freshly ground black pepper
2 whole heads of garlic
1 large orange
Sprigs of fresh rosemary to garnish

1 Put the poussins in a deep glass or china dish. Mix the oil with the vinegar, bay leaf, thyme, rosemary and orange rind and season with pepper. Pour the mixture over the poussins, cover and place in the refrigerator to marinate for 2-4 hours. Turn the poussins several times to keep coated with marinade.

2 Wrap the garlic heads separately in foil, and cook them in the heated oven for 25 minutes, or until tender.

3 Meanwhile, pare the rind thinly from the whole orange and cut into fine shreds. Pare off the pith and outer membrane from the flesh with a sharp knife, then slice out the segments, cutting each free of the membrane on either side. Work over a bowl to catch the juice.

4 Unwrap the garlic to cool, then remove the skins and crush the cloves to a paste with a fork. Lift the poussins out of the marinade and pat dry with kitchen paper. Carefully loosen the skin from the breast of each poussin, working from the neck end and pushing your fingers first along one side of the breast, then along the other. Spread the garlic purée evenly under the skin with a round-ended knife.

5 Place the poussins breast down on the grill rack and place the grill pan on its lowest position so the poussins will not char. Grill under a high heat for 10-12 minutes. Turn the poussins over and cook for 10-12 minutes more, until golden brown and cooked through. When they are pierced at the thickest part of the thigh with the tip of a knife the juice should run clear, not pink.

6 When the poussins are almost ready, simmer the finely shredded orange rind in the orange juice for 3-4 minutes.

7 Arrange the poussins on a heated serving plate and garnish with the orange segments, shreds and juice, and rosemary sprigs.

Divide the poussins with a sharp knife and give each diner a breast and a leg with some of the garnishes. Leave the diners to remove the chicken skin for themselves. Simple accompaniments such as french bread and a green salad suit the savoury poussins.

The surprisingly mild, nutty flavour of a garlic purée combines with piquant herbs and orange, making this a delicious dish for a summer lunch or dinner celebration.

Skinning the chicken pieces lets them absorb the contrasting flavours of cool grapefruit and hot peppercorns, and it lowers the fat content.

Chicken with pink grapefruit

ONE SERVING	
CALORIES	195
TOTAL FAT	8g
SATURATED FAT	2g
CARBOHYDRATES	12g
ADDED SUGAR	0
FIBRE	2g
SODIUM	100mg

SERVES 4
PREPARATION TIME: 20 minutes
COOKING TIME: 50 minutes

1 tablespoon olive oil
1 clove garlic, peeled and halved
8 chicken thighs, each about 3oz (85g), skinned
¼ pint (150ml) chicken stock
1 whole pink grapefruit and juice of another
1 level teaspoon pink peppercorns
1 medium onion, peeled and cut into thin strips
2 medium carrots, peeled and cut into thin strips
1 level teaspoon arrowroot
1 tablespoon water
Flat-leaf parsley to garnish

1 Heat the oil and garlic in a frying pan and cook the chicken thighs in it over a moderate heat for 5-6 minutes, turning them until golden all over. Pour in the stock and bring to the boil, then cook over a high heat for about 3 minutes, until the liquid is reduced by half. Add the grapefruit juice, peppercorns, onion and carrots to the pan, cover and cook over a moderate heat for 40 minutes.

2 Meanwhile, cut the skin and pith off the remaining grapefruit, then cut across the segments into eight slices.

3 Blend the arrowroot and water and stir it into the pan juices, simmering until they thicken slightly. Add the grapefruit slices and heat for 1 minute. Arrange on a hot serving dish and garnish with the parsley.

Rice and green beans complement the subtle taste of the chicken. You can make the dish with ordinary grapefruit but pink ones are sweeter as well as more attractive.

Oven-fried chicken

SERVES 4
PREPARATION TIME: 15 minutes, plus 30 minutes
to refrigerate
COOKING TIME: 30 minutes
OVEN: Preheat to 190°C (375°F, gas mark 5)

3 cloves garlic, peeled and crushed
1 level teaspoon dried thyme
1 level teaspoon dried marjoram
4oz (115g) low-fat natural yoghurt
4 boneless chicken breasts, each
about 6oz (175g), skinned
2oz (60g) fresh wholemeal breadcrumbs
2 level tablespoons chopped fresh parsley
3 level tablespoons grated Parmesan cheese
Young sprigs of thyme to garnish

1 Mix the garlic, thyme and marjoram into the
yoghurt and coat the chicken breasts with it.

2 On a flat plate, mix the breadcrumbs,
parsley and Parmesan. Press both sides of the
chicken breasts into the breadcrumb mixture,
then put them on a plate, cover and refrigerate
for 30 minutes for the coating to firm up.

3 Lay the chicken breasts on a nonstick baking
tray and cook in the heated oven for about
30 minutes, or until cooked right through with
no pink juices oozing out when the thickest
part of each chicken breast is pricked with a
fork. Lift the chicken onto a serving dish and
garnish with the thyme sprigs.

Serve the chicken with wild rice and some
cooked cranberries, very lightly sweetened, to
enhance the tangy flavour of the chicken.
A crisp green salad and perhaps some herb
bread will complete a satisfying dish.

ONE SERVING	
CALORIES	295
TOTAL FAT	8g
SATURATED FAT	3g
CARBOHYDRATES	15g
ADDED SUGAR	0
FIBRE	2g
SODIUM	315mg

TIP
*To make
breadcrumbs
without a food
processor, keep the
bread, unsliced, for
three or four days,
until very dry, then
rub firmly down
a sharp metal
grater.*

*The delicious herb,
cheese and breadcrumb
coating makes an
unusual meal out of
tender chicken breasts,
and seals in their juices
while they cook.*

Pan-fried chicken with cucumber

SERVES 4
PREPARATION TIME: 15 minutes
COOKING TIME: 20 minutes

1 large cucumber, halved lengthways and de-seeded
1 tablespoon olive oil
4 tablespoons water
1 small onion, peeled and finely chopped
4 boneless chicken breasts, each about 6oz (175g), skinned and cut into thin strips
Strained juice of 2 lemons
Strained juice of 1 lime
Freshly ground black pepper
Shredded and whole basil leaves to garnish

1 Peel some strips of skin off the cucumber halves, leaving them striped. Cut them into chunks, put in a saucepan and barely cover with water. Bring to the boil, then lower the heat and simmer, uncovered, for 3 minutes. Drain, put aside the cucumber and discard the water.

2 Heat the oil and water in a frying pan and cook the onion in it over a moderate heat for about 4 minutes, until the liquid has almost evaporated. Stir in the strips of chicken and fry for about 5 minutes, stirring until cooked through and golden.

3 Pour on the lemon and lime juice, made up to 7fl oz (200ml) with water. Season with pepper, bring to the boil, add the cucumber and simmer for 5-6 minutes. Spoon the chicken and sauce onto a hot serving plate and sprinkle with the basil shreds and sprigs.

Saffron rice and crisp, grated carrots go well with this fresh-flavoured dish.

ONE SERVING	
CALORIES	245
TOTAL FAT	8g
SATURATED FAT	2g
CARBOHYDRATES	4g
ADDED SUGAR	0
FIBRE	1g
SODIUM	130mg

TIP
To de-seed a cucumber, cut it in half lengthways and draw the tip of a teaspoon along firmly from end to end of each half.

The bite-sized pieces of chicken and faintly bitter cucumber in a lime and lemon sauce make this a refreshing dish for an outdoor summer lunch.

Chicken breasts Provençal

ONE SERVING
CALORIES 210
TOTAL FAT 7g
SATURATED FAT 2g
CARBOHYDRATES 9g
ADDED SUGAR 0
FIBRE 3g
SODIUM 185mg

SERVES 4
PREPARATION TIME: 10-15 minutes
COOKING TIME: 45 minutes

1 tablespoon olive oil
2 boneless chicken breasts, each about 8oz (225g), skinned and cut in half
1 large onion, peeled and chopped
4 cloves garlic, peeled and chopped
1 medium red pepper, de-seeded and diced

1 medium courgette, trimmed and sliced
1 small aubergine, trimmed and cut into chunks
14oz (400g) tinned chopped tomatoes
2 small red chillies
1/2 level teaspoon each dried basil, dried oregano, and dried thyme
4 large green olives, stoned and quartered
2 level tablespoons chopped fresh parsley

1 Heat the oil in a large, nonstick frying pan, and brown the chicken breasts in it over a moderate heat for 5 minutes on each side. Put them on a plate and set aside.

2 In the same pan, fry the onion and garlic for 5-6 minutes, stirring occasionally. Add the red pepper and cook for another 5 minutes, then add the courgette and cook for 5 minutes more. Put the vegetables with the chicken.

3 Using the same pan, toss the aubergine for 5-7 minutes, until browned. Return the chicken and vegetables to the pan. Stir in the tomatoes, chillies, basil, oregano, thyme and olives. Bring to the boil and then simmer for 15 minutes, or until the chicken is tender.

Arrange the chicken on a heated serving dish and spoon the vegetables round, discarding the chillies. Sprinkle the chopped parsley on top. Serve with crusty rolls to mop up the piquant sauce and a light, leafy salad to make a contrast.

Olives and chillies add a rich, fiery element to the South-of-France combination of tomatoes, peppers, aubergines and courgettes enveloping the chicken.

Sweet and sour apricot chicken

ONE SERVING
CALORIES 250
TOTAL FAT 8g
SATURATED FAT 2g
CARBOHYDRATES 14g
ADDED SUGAR 1g
FIBRE 2g
SODIUM 175mg

SERVES 4
PREPARATION TIME: 20 minutes
COOKING TIME: 50 minutes, plus
at least 30 minutes to marinate
OVEN: Preheat to 200°C (400°F, gas mark 6)

2 tablespoons lemon juice
2 teaspoons olive oil
2 cloves garlic, peeled and crushed
Freshly ground black pepper

2 1/2 -3lb (1.1-1.4kg) chicken, divided
into 8 portions and skinned
3oz (85g) ready-to-use dried apricots
7fl oz (200ml) unsweetened orange juice
1 level teaspoon light brown sugar
1 tablespoon cider vinegar
2 level teaspoons peeled and grated root ginger,
or 1/4 level teaspoon ground ginger
1 level teaspoon Dijon mustard
Bay leaves to garnish

1 Mix the lemon juice with the oil and half the garlic, and season with pepper. Put the chicken in a dish, pour on the lemon marinade and turn the chicken pieces in it until thoroughly coated. Cover and leave in a cool place for at least 30 minutes or up to 2 hours, turning the chicken several times.

2 Meanwhile, simmer the apricots in the orange juice for 10 minutes, or until tender. Stir in the sugar, vinegar, ginger, mustard and remaining garlic. Simmer for another 2 minutes. Cool the mixture slightly, then liquidise it in a food processor for 15 seconds or pass it through a food mill.

3 Arrange the chicken portions in a single layer on a rack in a roasting tin and cook in the heated oven for 25 minutes.

The tartness of apricots, sharpened by the juice of citrus fruits, gives this dish its distinctive flavour. A trace of ginger in the attractive golden glaze reinforces the association with favourites from a Chinese cook's repertoire.

4 Brush over one side of the chicken pieces with half the apricot glaze and roast for 10 more minutes. Turn the pieces over, brush the other side with the remaining glaze and roast 10 minutes longer, or until the chicken is tender and the glaze lightly browned.

Serve the chicken with a garnish of bay leaves. Rice and mangetout go well with it. Give each diner a breast portion and a leg portion. You can use four chicken legs, divided into thighs and drumsticks, instead of a jointed chicken.

The spicy marinade permeating this chicken re-creates the authentic flavour of a classic Indian dish, which is traditionally cooked in a tandoor, a clay oven, over a charcoal fire.

Tandoori chicken

SERVES 4
PREPARATION TIME: 15 minutes, plus
at least 4 hours to marinate
COOKING TIME: 30 minutes
OVEN: Preheat to 180°C (350°F, gas mark 4)

4oz (115g) Greek yoghurt
1 small onion, peeled and very finely chopped
1 level tablespoon peeled and grated root ginger,
or ¹/₂ level teaspoon ground ginger
2 cloves garlic, peeled and crushed
1 tablespoon lime juice
1¹/₂ level teaspoons ground coriander
1 level teaspoon each ground cumin, ground
cardamom and turmeric
¹/₄ level teaspoon cayenne pepper
1 level tablespoon paprika
4 chicken breast and wing portions, each
about 8oz (225g), skinned
Lime wedges and parsley to garnish

1 Blend the yoghurt, onion, ginger, garlic and
lime juice in a food processor for 30 seconds, or
combine them with a rotary hand whisk. Mix in
the coriander, cumin, cardamom, turmeric,
cayenne pepper and paprika. Pour into a large,
glass or china dish, put in the chicken pieces
and turn to coat with the yoghurt mixture.
Cover and refrigerate for at least 4 hours or up
to 24 hours, turning to recoat occasionally.

2 Heat the grill, arrange the chicken on the
grill rack and cook under a moderate heat for
8 minutes on each side, until browned.

3 Put the chicken pieces in a nonstick baking
tin and cook in the heated oven for about
15 minutes or until the juices run clear when
the chicken is pierced with a sharp knife.

4 Lift the chicken onto a warm serving plate
and garnish with the lime wedges and parsley.

TIP
For the fullest and freshest flavour from the spices, grind your own coriander, cumin and cardamom seeds as you need them, using a mortar and pestle.

ONE SERVING	
CALORIES 190	
TOTAL FAT 7g	
SATURATED FAT 3g	
CARBOHYDRATES 2g	
ADDED SUGAR 0	
FIBRE 1g	
SODIUM 110mg	

Duck satay

TIP
If you are using wooden skewers, soak them in cold water for 15-20 minutes before threading the meat on them. This helps to prevent them from scorching.

SERVES 4
PREPARATION TIME: 10 minutes, plus 2 hours to marinate
COOKING TIME: 10 minutes
OVEN: Preheat to 200°C (400°F, gas mark 6)

½ level teaspoon ground ginger
1 tablespoon soy sauce
1 teaspoon Worcestershire sauce
Finely grated rind and juice of 2 oranges
Freshly ground black pepper
1lb (450g) duck breast, without skin or bone, cubed
4 long wooden or metal skewers
2oz (60g) unsalted cashew nuts
Orange wedges, strips of rind and parsley to garnish

1 Mix the ginger, soy sauce, Worcestershire sauce and orange rind and juice in a glass or china casserole, and season with pepper. Stir in the duck, cover and refrigerate for 2 hours.

2 Thread the duck onto the skewers. Put them in a roasting tin, spoon on the marinade and cook in the heated oven for about 10 minutes, or until the duck is cooked through and tender.

3 Meanwhile spread the cashew nuts on a baking tray and roast in the oven for 5 minutes, until golden brown. Set aside.

4 When the duck is cooked, lift the skewers onto a heated serving dish, cover and keep hot.

5 Put the cashew nuts into a food processor with the cooking juices from the duck and blend until smooth. Reheat, put into a warmed serving bowl and top with strips of orange rind.

Serve the duck satay with rice and garnish with orange wedges and parsley. Stir-fried mangetout make a crisp accompaniment.

In this adaptation of a traditional South-east Asian dish, the marinaded and skewered meat is roasted and its juices are added to the spicy nut sauce.

BEEF, LAMB AND PORK

Red meat is invaluable for the complete protein, vitamins and minerals it contributes to the diet, but these go hand in hand with the saturated fats that should be avoided. The knack is to make a little meat go a long way, and these recipes show how to do it. They skilfully use prudent portions in delicious dishes, cooked by roasting and stewing and by quick grilling and stir-frying to cut down fat but keep flavour intact.

Beefburgers Scandinavian style

SERVES 4
PREPARATION TIME: 10 minutes, plus 20 minutes to chill
COOKING TIME: 15 minutes

12oz (340g) beef with fat removed, minced
3oz (85g) cooked beetroot, peeled and diced
2oz (60g) fresh wholemeal breadcrumbs

1 egg, size 3, beaten
2 teaspoons red wine vinegar
½ level teaspoon dried dill
Freshly ground black pepper
1 tablespoon olive oil
Shredded lettuce, onion rings and dill fronds to garnish
Soured cream to garnish

1 Combine the beef, beetroot, breadcrumbs, egg, vinegar and dried dill, and season with pepper. Divide the mixture into four, shape into flat cakes and refrigerate for 20 minutes.

2 Heat the oil in a frying pan and brown the beefburgers over a high heat for 1-2 minutes on each side. Lower the heat to moderate and cook the burgers for 5 minutes more on each side.

3 Drain the beefburgers on kitchen paper before arranging them on individual plates and garnishing with the lettuce, onion and dill. Hand the soured cream round for the diners to put a teaspoonful on their burger; you can mix a little chopped dill with the cream.

Beetroot gives the beefburgers a rich colour and a hint of sweetness which is offset by soured cream in a favourite Scandinavian combination.

Beef wrapped in cabbage leaves

SERVES 4
PREPARATION TIME: 40 minutes
COOKING TIME: 25 minutes
OVEN: Preheat to 200°C (400°F, gas mark 6)

1 tablespoon olive oil
1 large clove garlic, peeled and crushed
1 small red onion, peeled and finely chopped
2 rashers unsmoked back bacon, trimmed of fat and chopped
1lb (450g) beef with fat removed, minced
Sprig fresh oregano

3 basil leaves, chopped, or ¼ level teaspoon dried basil
¼ level teaspoon freshly grated nutmeg or ground nutmeg
Freshly ground black pepper
1 level teaspoon arrowroot
1 tablespoon balsamic vinegar
3fl oz (85ml) unsweetened red grape juice
14oz (400g) tinned chopped tomatoes
8 large savoy cabbage leaves
8oz (225g) cooked borlotti or black-eyed beans

1 Heat the oil in a large frying pan and toss the garlic and onion in it over a high heat for 1 minute. Add the bacon and cook for 1 minute. Stir in the beef and fry for about 10 minutes until brown, breaking up any lumps that form. Stir in the oregano, basil and nutmeg, and season with pepper.

2 Blend the arrowroot with the vinegar and grape juice and stir into the minced-beef mixture until the juices come to the boil and thicken. Pour in the tomatoes and simmer, covered, for 20 minutes.

3 Meanwhile bring a large saucepan of water to the boil and cook the cabbage for 2 minutes, then rinse with cold water and drain.

4 Mix the beans into the beef thoroughly, then turn the mixture into a sieve set over a bowl

and discard the oregano. Let the juices drain out and keep them for the sauce.

5 Lay the cabbage leaves inside up on a board. Spoon the beef mixture onto the leaves, fold the sides in over the filling and roll the leaves up firmly. Arrange the rolls, seam side down, in one layer in a casserole. Add 2-3 tablespoons of water, put on the lid and bake in the heated oven for about 20 minutes, or until the leaf ribs are just tender.

6 Bring the reserved juices to the boil in a small saucepan while you lift the cabbage rolls onto a heated serving dish. Pour the sauce round them.

A tomato gratin and mashed potato with swede add colour and varied texture to the parcels of beef and beans.

Deep green, crinkly leaves of the savoy cabbage make attractive, crisp wrappings for a substantial, well-flavoured beef and bean filling.

Beef parcels with chestnuts and red wine

SERVES 4
PREPARATION TIME: 30 minutes
COOKING TIME: 1 hour
OVEN: Preheat to 160°C (325°F, gas mark 3)

4oz (115g) chestnuts, shell and inner skin removed,
finely chopped
2oz (60g) mushrooms, wiped and finely chopped
1 small carrot, peeled and grated
1 clove garlic, peeled and crushed
1 level tablespoon whole-grain mustard
2 level teaspoons chopped fresh thyme
⅛ level teaspoon salt
Freshly ground black pepper
4 slices braising beef, each about 4oz (115g),
fat removed, beaten out thin
Thin string to tie parcels
1 tablespoon olive oil
3 shallots or small onions, peeled and finely sliced
1 level tablespoon plain flour
¼ pint (150ml) red wine
¼ pint (150ml) vegetable or beef stock

1 Mix together thoroughly the chestnuts, mushrooms, carrot, garlic, mustard, thyme and salt, and season with pepper. Spread out the beef slices on a board and spoon a quarter of the chestnut mixture onto the centre of each. Wrap the meat round the stuffing to make four neat parcels and tie with clean, thin string.

2 Heat the oil in a flameproof casserole and brown the parcels in it over a high heat. Lift them out with a slotted spoon and set aside. Cook the shallots or onions in the casserole gently for 2-3 minutes. Stir in the flour and cook for 1 minute, then gradually stir in the wine and stock and continue stirring while the sauce comes to the boil and thickens.

3 Return the beef parcels to the casserole, cover and cook in the heated oven for 1 hour. Carefully snip and remove the string when you serve the parcels.

Cauliflower, baked tomatoes and jacket potatoes go well with the moist beef parcels. You can use ale in place of the wine and, when chestnuts are out of season, soaked and chopped dried chestnuts can replace them. If you gather your own chestnuts, be sure they are sweet chestnuts, not horse chestnuts.

ONE SERVING	
CALORIES	275
TOTAL FAT	10g
SATURATED FAT	3g
CARBOHYDRATES	16g
ADDED SUGAR	0
FIBRE	2g
SODIUM	140mg

TIP
Chestnuts peel
easily if you cut a
deep cross in the top
of each, put them in
a pan with cold
water to cover,
bring to the boil
and simmer for
10 minutes. Spoon
out one at a time
to peel.

The sweet chestnut stuffing and the rich wine sauce are delicious accompaniments to the thinly beaten slices of beef. They combine to make an unusual autumn dish.

Beef kebabs with courgettes and tomatoes

SERVES 4
*PREPARATION TIME: 20 minutes, plus 3 hours
to marinate*
COOKING TIME: 15 minutes

4 level tablespoons low-fat natural yoghurt
2 tablespoons lemon juice
2 cloves garlic, peeled and finely chopped
*2 level teaspoons peeled and grated root ginger,
or ½ level teaspoon ground ginger*
2 level teaspoons paprika
*½ level teaspoon each cayenne pepper, ground
nutmeg, cumin and coriander*
*1lb (450g) rump steak with fat removed,
cut into 12 cubes*
1 medium courgette, trimmed and cut into 12 slices
*1 large red pepper, de-seeded and cut
into 12 squares*
4 long metal skewers
8 cherry tomatoes
2 small onions, peeled and cut into quarters
Fresh coriander leaves to garnish

1 Mix the yoghurt, lemon juice, garlic and
ginger with the paprika, cayenne pepper,
nutmeg, cumin and coriander. Whisk the
mixture well, or blend it in a food processor
for 10 seconds.

2 Pour the mixture into a glass or china bowl
and turn the beef cubes in it to coat well. Cover
and put in the refrigerator for 3 hours to
marinate. Turn the meat once during this time.

3 Blanch the courgette and pepper for one
minute in boiling water.

4 Lift the beef cubes out of the marinade and
thread onto four oiled skewers, with a share of
the courgette, red pepper, tomatoes and onion.
Lay the kebabs on the grill rack and cook under
a high heat for 15-20 minutes, frequently
brushing with the marinade and turning until
the meat and vegetables are tender. Reduce the
heat if the kebabs are browning too much.

*Marinating meat in yoghurt and lemon juice makes
it a fittingly tender partner for the vegetables in this
colourful dish. Here the yoghurt is warmly spiced.*

Serve the kebabs very hot, still on their skewers,
on a bed of boiled green lentils and garnished
with fresh coriander. A dish of diced cucumber
mixed with low-fat natural yoghurt is a
welcome cool accompaniment to the spicy
kebabs. For a summer meal, you might prefer
rolls and a leafy salad with the kebabs.

ONE SERVING	
CALORIES	185
TOTAL FAT	6g
SATURATED FAT	3g
CARBOHYDRATES	8g
ADDED SUGAR	0
FIBRE	1g
SODIUM	90mg

Spanish-style spiced beef

SERVES 4
PREPARATION TIME: 15 minutes
COOKING TIME: 45 minutes

12oz (340g) chuck steak with fat removed, minced
1 large Spanish onion, peeled and chopped
1 small green pepper, de-seeded and chopped
2 cloves garlic, peeled and crushed
1½ level teaspoons chilli powder
14oz (400g) tinned chopped tomatoes, drained
with 3fl oz (85ml) of their juice reserved
1oz (30g) raisins
2 tablespoons cider vinegar
2 teaspoons tomato purée
½ level teaspoon ground ginger
½ level teaspoon dried thyme
Freshly ground black pepper
1 small cos-type lettuce, cleaned and shredded
4 spring onions, trimmed
8-12 small radishes, trimmed and halved
3½ oz (100g) low-fat natural yoghurt

1 Cook the beef in a dry frying pan over a moderate heat for 3-5 minutes, stirring it to break up any lumps, until it is no longer pink.

2 Stir in the onion, green pepper, garlic and 1 teaspoon of the chilli powder, and continue cooking and stirring for 8 minutes.

3 Mix in the tomatoes and juice, the raisins, vinegar, tomato purée, ginger and thyme, and season with pepper. Simmer gently, uncovered, for 30 minutes, stirring occasionally.

4 Spread the lettuce on serving plates, pile a share of the beef on top and garnish with the spring onions and radishes. Stir the yoghurt until smooth, sprinkle the remaining chilli powder on it and hand round separately.

Wholemeal bread and a salad of green beans and courgettes are satisfying accompaniments.

ONE SERVING	
CALORIES	195
TOTAL FAT	5g
SATURATED FAT	2g
CARBOHYDRATES	17g
ADDED SUGAR	0
FIBRE	3g
SODIUM	145mg

TIP
To minimise the fat, buy chuck steak, or if not available beef skirt, and mince it yourself after cutting off the fat. If you do not have a mincer, ask the butcher to trim and mince the meat.

The crunchy salad ingredients in this dish make a refreshing contrast to the spicy beef and a spoonful of yoghurt cools it.

Stir-frying seals in the beef's juices and keeps the vegetables crisp. You can serve the dish with egg noodles to complete the Chinese theme.

Beef stir-fry

ONE SERVING

CALORIES 235

TOTAL FAT 10g

SATURATED FAT 2g

CARBOHYDRATES 12g

ADDED SUGAR 0

FIBRE 3g

SODIUM 160mg

TIP
Chilling the beef in the freezer for 20-25 minutes makes it easier to cut into thin strips.

SERVES 4
PREPARATION TIME: 10 minutes
COOKING TIME: 15 minutes

1 tablespoon vegetable oil
12oz (340g) rump steak, cut into matchstick strips
1 large onion, peeled and sliced
1 green or red pepper, de-seeded and cut into strips
1 large carrot, peeled and cut into matchstick strips
8fl oz (225ml) beef stock
8oz (225g) button mushrooms, wiped and sliced
4fl oz (115ml) dry white wine
1 level tablespoon cornflour
2 tablespoons water
1 teaspoon soy sauce
1 teaspoon sesame oil
6oz (175g) bean sprouts

1 Heat the oil in a heavy-based frying pan and stir-fry the steak in it over a high heat for 1 minute. Use a slotted spoon to lift the steak onto a plate.

2 Stir-fry the onion, pepper and carrot in the pan with 2 tablespoons of stock for 1 minute.

3 Add the mushrooms, wine and remaining stock and simmer for 3 minutes. Blend the cornflour with the water and stir into the pan juices until the sauce thickens. Cook gently for 2 minutes.

4 Stir in the soy sauce, sesame oil and bean sprouts and return the meat to the pan. Cook for 1 minute. Serve at once while piping hot.

Lamb and asparagus stir-fry

SERVES 4
PREPARATION TIME: 20 minutes, plus 30 minutes
to marinate
COOKING TIME: 15 minutes

ONE SERVING
CALORIES 330
TOTAL FAT 18g
    SATURATED FAT 5g
CARBOHYDRATES 12g
    ADDED SUGAR 0
FIBRE 3g
SODIUM 660mg

2 level tablespoons peeled and grated root ginger,
or 1 level teaspoon ground ginger
2 cloves garlic, peeled and crushed
2 tablespoons soy sauce
2 tablespoons dry sherry
2 tablespoons sesame oil
1lb (450g) lamb without bone or fat, cut into strips
1lb (450g) thin asparagus, trimmed and cut
diagonally into short lengths

1 Spanish onion, peeled, quartered and sliced
1 medium green pepper, de-seeded and sliced
1 level teaspoon cornflour
3fl oz (85ml) chicken or vegetable stock
3oz (85g) bamboo shoots
3oz (85g) water chestnuts, thinly sliced

1 Combine the ginger, garlic, soy sauce, sherry
and 1 teaspoon of the sesame oil in a glass or
china dish. Stir the lamb into this marinade,
cover and leave in a cool place for 30 minutes.

2 Heat 1 tablespoon of the sesame oil in
a large frying pan over a high heat and stir-fry
the asparagus in it for 3-5 minutes until just
becoming tender. Add the onion and green
pepper and stir-fry for 1 minute more, then
cover and cook for 1 minute. Using a slotted
spoon, lift all the vegetables onto a large plate.

3 Heat the remaining sesame oil in the pan
over a high heat and stir in the lamb. Pour on
the marinade and cook, stirring, for 5 minutes.
Blend the cornflour with the stock, stir into the
pan juices and boil until the liquid thickens.

4 Put the vegetables back in the pan, mix in
the bamboo shoots and water chestnuts
and toss over a moderate heat for 2 minutes.

Serve the stir-fry while piping hot with plenty
of fluffed-up rice.

*Young asparagus stalks are ideal for stir-frying and
their delicate flavour suits that of the lamb. Bamboo
shoots and water chestnuts add satisfying crunchiness.*

Lamb baked in aubergines

ONE SERVING
CALORIES 195
TOTAL FAT 9g
    SATURATED FAT 4g
CARBOHYDRATES 8g
    ADDED SUGAR 0
FIBRE 3g
SODIUM 185mg

SERVES 4
PREPARATION TIME: 20 minutes, plus 30 minutes
to stand
COOKING TIME: 1 hour 5 minutes
OVEN: Preheat to 190°C (375°F, gas mark 5)

2 medium aubergines
¼ level teaspoon salt
1 teaspoon olive oil
1 onion, peeled and chopped

2 cloves garlic, peeled and chopped
12oz (340g) lamb without bone or fat, minced
1 level teaspoon each ground cumin and coriander
2 level teaspoons plain flour
7oz (200g) tinned chopped tomatoes
1oz (30g) pine nuts, lightly toasted
2 level tablespoons chopped fresh parsley
Freshly ground black pepper
2 level tablespoons fresh brown breadcrumbs
Lime wedges and coriander sprigs to garnish

Aubergines acting as edible gratin dishes provide a tinge of bitterness to offset the sweetness of the filling.

1 Halve the aubergines lengthways, score the cut surfaces crisscross fashion, sprinkle with the salt and leave to stand for 30 minutes.

2 Rinse the aubergines with plenty of cold water, pat them dry and put them cut side down on a sheet of nonstick baking paper on a baking sheet. Prick the skin all over and bake in the heated oven for 30 minutes.

3 Meanwhile, heat the oil in a heavy-based saucepan and toss the onion and garlic in it over a high heat until golden. Stir in the lamb and cook briskly until it begins to brown. Break up any lumps that form with a fork.

4 Sprinkle on the cumin, coriander and flour and cook, stirring, for 30 seconds. Pour in the tomatoes and bring to the boil, then stir, cover and simmer for about 10 minutes.

5 When the aubergines are tender, scoop out the flesh leaving shells about ¼ in (6mm) thick. Chop the flesh and stir it into the lamb along with the pine nuts and chopped parsley. Season the mixture with pepper.

6 Fill the aubergine shells with the lamb mixture, arrange them in an ovenproof dish and sprinkle on the breadcrumbs. Pour a thin covering of water into the bottom of the dish. Bake the filled aubergines in the heated oven for about 50 minutes, or until they are crisp and golden brown on top.

Garnish the aubergines with the lime wedges and coriander and serve with bulgur wheat simmered with a few sultanas to emphasise the Balkan flavour of the dish. Side salads of tomato and onion sprinkled with snipped dill fronds or parsley will provide a sharp contrast.

Lamb curry

ONE SERVING

CALORIES 325

TOTAL FAT 15g

SATURATED FAT 6g

CARBOHYDRATES 21g

ADDED SUGAR 0

FIBRE 5g

SODIUM 160mg

TIP
You will find it quicker to brown the cubes of lamb a few at a time so the heat in the pan remains high.

SERVES 4
PREPARATION TIME: 25 minutes
COOKING TIME: 55 minutes

1 tablespoon corn oil
1lb (450g) meat from boned chump ends or neck fillet of lamb, fat removed, cut into small cubes
1 medium onion, peeled and thinly sliced
½ small stick celery, trimmed and thinly sliced
1 clove garlic, peeled and crushed
1-2 level tablespoons curry powder
½ level teaspoon each ground cumin, ground cardamom and ground coriander
1 small carrot, peeled and grated
4fl oz (115ml) beef stock
¼ level teaspoon cayenne pepper
1 cooking apple, unpeeled, cored and cut into cubes
8oz (225g) small okra or fine green beans, trimmed
2oz (60g) raisins
4oz (115g) low-fat natural yoghurt

1 Heat the oil in a large, heavy-based frying pan and brown the lamb cubes in it on all sides over a high heat. Use a slotted spoon to lift the meat out and put it to drain on kitchen paper.

2 Cook the onion, celery and garlic gently in the frying pan for 5 minutes, stirring frequently. Add the curry powder, cumin, cardamom and coriander and stir for 1 minute. Stir in the lamb, carrot, stock or water and cayenne pepper. Cover and simmer for 40 minutes, or until the lamb is tender.

3 Mix in the apple, okra or beans, and raisins, and a little water if necessary. Cover and cook for 5 minutes, or until the okra is tender.

4 Blend in the yoghurt and heat, taking care not to boil or it will curdle.

Brown or basmati rice and a side dish of thinly sliced tomatoes and onion rings, or coarsely grated carrots would go well with the curry. You can add a garnish of parsley or coriander sprigs for a fresh touch of colour.

Raisins accentuate the tender sweetness of the lamb, striking a perfect balance with the hot, savoury curry spices and sharp, crisp apple.

In common with all pulses, flageolet beans are a good source of fibre; their delicate flavour and tender skin make them a subtle and satisfying partner for the lamb in this colourful dish.

Braised lamb chops with flageolet beans

ONE SERVING	
CALORIES	355
TOTAL FAT	15g
SATURATED FAT	6g
CARBOHYDRATES	26g
ADDED SUGAR	0
FIBRE	8g
SODIUM	190mg

SERVES 4
PREPARATION TIME: 25 minutes
COOKING TIME: 40 minutes
OVEN: Preheat to 180°C (350°F, gas mark 4)

1 tablespoon olive oil
4 lamb chump chops, each about 6oz (175g), fat removed
2 cloves garlic, peeled and chopped
2 onions, peeled and chopped
3 sticks celery, trimmed and sliced
2 carrots, peeled and sliced
14oz (400g) tinned chopped tomatoes
2 tablespoons tomato purée
2 level teaspoons dried rosemary, finely crumbled
2 level teaspoons paprika
1 level teaspoon Dijon mustard or made English mustard
12oz (340g) cooked flageolet beans
Freshly ground black pepper
Flat-leaf parsley to garnish

1 Heat the oil in a flameproof casserole and brown the chops in it over a high heat for 2-3 minutes on each side. Lift the chops onto kitchen paper to drain.

2 Brown the garlic, onions, celery and carrots in the casserole over a moderate heat for about 5 minutes, stirring occasionally. Mix in the tomatoes and their juice, the tomato purée, rosemary, paprika and mustard. Gently mix in the flageolet beans, season with pepper and bring the casserole to the boil.

3 Arrange the chops on top of the vegetables, put the lid on the casserole and cook in the heated oven for about 40 minutes, or until the lamb is tender.

Serve crusty bread with the dish. A garnish of parsley and a side dish of peppery kale or savoy cabbage give a contrast in flavour and colour.

Herbed lamb cutlets

SERVES 4
PREPARATION TIME: 5 minutes
COOKING TIME: 8 minutes

8 lamb cutlets, each about 4oz (115g), fat trimmed
2 cloves garlic, peeled and halved
1 tablespoon olive oil
1 level tablespoon chopped mixed fresh thyme,
marjoram and rosemary, or 1 level teaspoon dried
mixed herbs
Freshly ground black pepper
Fresh mint and lemon wedges to garnish

1 Lay the cutlets in a shallow dish and rub all over with the cut side of the garlic cloves. Brush both sides of the cutlets with the oil, coat with the herbs and season with pepper.

2 Place the cutlets on the grill rack and cook under a high heat for 4 minutes on each side. Arrange them on warmed serving plates and garnish with the mint and lemon.

Serve with new potatoes and a green salad, and let the diners remove any remaining fat.

TIP
To enhance the herb flavour of the cutlets, coat them 4-5 hours before cooking, cover the dish and put in the refrigerator to marinate.

For ease of preparation and freshness of taste, nothing beats young and tender lamb cutlets briefly grilled in a coating of lively herbs.

Lamb and lentil shepherd's pie

SERVES 4
PREPARATION TIME: 35 minutes
COOKING TIME: 20 minutes
OVEN: Preheat to 200°C (400°F, gas mark 6)

3oz (85g) green lentils
1 tablespoon olive oil
1 medium onion, peeled and chopped
1 clove garlic, peeled and crushed
12oz (340g) boned leg of lamb, trimmed of fat and minced
2 small carrots, peeled and diced
2oz (60g) mushrooms, wiped and chopped
2oz (60g) frozen sweetcorn kernels
1 level teaspoon chopped fresh rosemary, or ½ level teaspoon dried rosemary

1 level teaspoon chopped fresh mint, or ½ level teaspoon dried mint
1 tablespoon tomato purée
14oz (400g) tinned chopped tomatoes
1½ lb (680g) potatoes, peeled and cut up
4 tablespoons skimmed milk
⅛ level teaspoon salt
Freshly ground black pepper

1 Cook the lentils and drain

2 Meanwhile, heat the oil in a large saucepan and toss the onion and garlic in it over a high heat for 2 minutes, until lightly browned. Stir in the lamb and cook for about 5 minutes, until the meat is no longer pink, breaking up any lumps with a fork.

3 Mix in the carrots, mushrooms, sweetcorn, rosemary and mint and cook for 2 minutes, then add the tomato purée and the tomatoes with their juice. Cover the saucepan and simmer for 20 minutes.

4 Boil or steam the potatoes until soft. Drain and mash them, then add the milk and beat until smooth. Cover and set aside.

5 Uncover the pan of lamb and vegetables and cook more briskly for 5 minutes to evaporate some of the liquid. Stir in the cooked lentils and salt, and season with pepper.

6 Turn the lamb mixture into an ovenproof dish, spread the potato over the top and mark with a fork. Cook in the heated oven for about 20 minutes, until golden brown.

Peas and carrots go particularly well with the sweet flavour of the lamb. Instead of lamb you can use lean minced beef, seasoned with 1 teaspoon of prepared mustard and ½ teaspoon dried thyme, or lean minced pork seasoned with 1 teaspoon dried sage and ½ teaspoon dried marjoram.

This variation of the traditional recipe is packed with colourful lentils, tomatoes and sweetcorn, making it a good source of fibre and a substantial, warming dish.

ONE SERVING

CALORIES 425

TOTAL FAT 13g

SATURATED FAT 4g

CARBOHYDRATES 52g

ADDED SUGAR 0

FIBRE 6g —

SODIUM 215mg

Indonesian-style pork kebabs

SERVES 4
PREPARATION TIME: 20 minutes, plus 1 hour
to marinate
COOKING TIME: 20 minutes

ONE SERVING	
CALORIES 205	
TOTAL FAT 11g	
SATURATED FAT 2g	
CARBOHYDRATES 5g	
ADDED SUGAR 3g	
FIBRE 1g	
SODIUM 160mg	

½ level teaspoon ground ginger
2 cloves garlic, peeled
1 small onion, peeled and chopped
1 teaspoon soy sauce
2 level tablespoons unsalted peanuts, toasted
1 teaspoon olive oil
2 level teaspoons soft brown sugar

2 teaspoons lemon juice
½ level teaspoon each ground coriander, cumin
and cinnamon
2 tablespoons water
12oz (340g) pork tenderloin, trimmed of fat and
cut into cubes
4 metal or wooden skewers
Finely shredded lemon rind, spring onion and
parsley leaves to garnish

1 Put the ginger, garlic, onion, soy sauce,
peanuts, oil, sugar, lemon juice, coriander,
cumin and cinnamon in a food processor with
the water. Blend for 8-10 seconds, until
smooth, then pour into a glass or china dish.
Stir the pork cubes into the mixture, cover and
put in the refrigerator to marinate for 1 hour.

2 Thread the meat onto the skewers, ensuring
that the cubes do not touch one another.

3 Lay the kebabs on a grill rack and brush
them with the marinade. Grill for about
20 minutes under a high heat, turning and
brushing with the marinade several times, until
the pork is cooked through. Arrange the kebabs
on a heated serving dish and garnish with the
lemon rind, spring onion and parsley.

Boiled rice provides a simple base for the richly
flavoured meat, and a crunchy bean sprout and
pepper salad refreshes the palate.

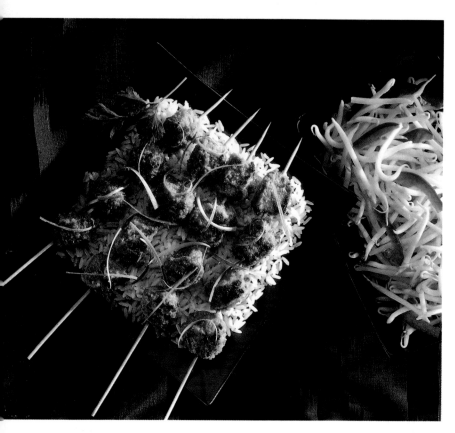

*The spicy peanut marinade gives an exotic taste of
the East to beautifully tender morsels of pork grilled
on skewers to brown every side to perfection.*

Stuffed loin of pork

ONE SERVING	
CALORIES 345	
TOTAL FAT 14g	
SATURATED FAT 4g	
CARBOHYDRATES 12g	
ADDED SUGAR 0	
FIBRE 2g	
SODIUM 185mg	

SERVES 4
PREPARATION TIME: 25 minutes
COOKING TIME: 45 minutes
OVEN: Preheat to 200°C (400°F, gas mark 6)

2 tablespoons olive oil
2 tablespoons water
1 large onion, peeled and chopped
1 large carrot, peeled and finely chopped

1 medium red pepper, de-seeded and finely chopped
Freshly ground black pepper
1oz (30g) wholemeal breadcrumbs
1 level teaspoon ground ginger
⅛ level teaspoon ground cloves
1½ lb (680g) rolled loin of pork, trimmed of fat
2 tablespoons lemon juice
7fl oz (200ml) vegetable or chicken
stock

The pork is trimmed of fat but, moistened from within by a savoury stuffing and from outside by stock, it cooks to tempting succulence.

1 Heat one tablespoon of the oil in a frying pan with the water and cook the onion, carrot and red pepper in it over a low heat for 6-8 minutes, until the vegetables are soft. Season with black pepper and stir in the breadcrumbs, ginger and cloves to make a well-blended stuffing.

2 Cut a pocket in the centre of the pork for the filling. Push in the stuffing, but not too tightly or it will be squeezed out as the meat shrinks during cooking. Sprinkle the lemon juice over the meat and rub it in well.

3 Heat the remaining oil in a small roasting tin over a moderately high direct heat and quickly brown the stuffed pork all over. Pour the stock in with the meat and bring it to the boil, then put the tin in the heated oven and cook the pork for 20 minutes. Lower the heat to 180°C (350°F, gas mark 4) and cook for another 20 minutes, basting from time to time with the stock, until the pork is cooked through.

4 Lift the pork onto a hot serving plate, cover it loosely with foil and leave it to rest for 10 minutes. Skim off and discard the fat from the juices in the roasting tin.

5 Reheat the roasting juices while you cut the meat into slices. Spoon the juices round the meat before serving.

New potatoes, mangetout and tiny sweetcorn cobs add bite and extra colour to the tender slices of pork.

TIP
To make the pocket for the stuffing, push a very sharp long-bladed knife through the centre of the meat from end to end. Move the knife gently from side to side until the slit is large enough to hold the stuffing.

Apple and cider, popular ingredients in the cooking of Normandy, mellow the lively herb flavouring in the sauce as well as the meatballs.

Normandy meatballs and cider sauce

ONE SERVING	
CALORIES	340
TOTAL FAT	14g
SATURATED FAT	5g
CARBOHYDRATES	21g
ADDED SUGAR	0
FIBRE	3g
SODIUM	295mg

SERVES 4
PREPARATION TIME: 15 minutes
COOKING TIME: 25 minutes
OVEN: Preheat to 200°C (400°F, gas mark 6)

1lb (450g) boneless pork with fat removed, minced
3oz (85g) wholemeal breadcrumbs
2oz (60g) ready-to-use stoned prunes, finely chopped
1 dessert apple, about 4oz (115g), peeled, cored and finely chopped
1oz (30g) walnuts, chopped
1 level tablespoon coarsely chopped fresh sage, or 1 level teaspoon dried sage
⅛ level teaspoon salt
Freshly ground black pepper
1 egg, size 2, lightly beaten
½ oz (15g) slightly salted butter
1 small onion, peeled and finely chopped
1 level tablespoon plain flour
¼ pint (150ml) vegetable or chicken stock
¼ pint (150ml) medium sweet cider
1 level tablespoon chopped fresh parsley
2 level tablespoons low-fat natural yoghurt
Sage leaves to garnish

1 Mix the pork, breadcrumbs, prunes, apple, walnuts and sage, season with salt and pepper and work in the egg to bind the mixture. Divide it into 20 pieces and roll each into a ball.

2 Put the pork balls into a nonstick roasting tin and cook in the heated oven for about 25 minutes, or until golden brown.

3 Meanwhile, melt the butter in a saucepan, and cook the onion in it gently for about 5 minutes, or until soft. Stir in the flour and cook for 30 seconds. Gradually stir in the stock and cider and bring to the boil, stirring continuously. Mix in the parsley, season with pepper and set the sauce aside.

4 When the meatballs are cooked, stir the yoghurt into the sauce and reheat, but do not boil or it will curdle. Pour into a warmed jug for serving. Turn the meatballs into a serving dish and garnish with sage leaves.

Mashed potato goes well with the meatballs, while crisp spring greens or broccoli will make a pleasing contrast with their tenderness.

Pork with roasted peppers

SERVES 4
PREPARATION TIME: 30 minutes
COOKING TIME: 25 minutes

ONE SERVING	
CALORIES	300
TOTAL FAT	9g
SATURATED FAT	2g
CARBOHYDRATES	27g
ADDED SUGAR	0
FIBRE	4g
SODIUM	185mg

Roasting the sweet red peppers enhances their characteristically smoky flavour. Partnered by tomatoes and sharpened by a little vinegar and cayenne, they give a vivid touch of the hot south to the pork.

2 large red peppers
1lb (450g) boned shoulder of pork with fat removed, cut into 4 slices
1 level tablespoon plain flour
1 tablespoon olive oil
1 medium onion, peeled and chopped
2 cloves garlic, peeled and crushed
2lb (900g) tinned tomatoes, drained and chopped
2oz (60g) sultanas
1 tablespoon red wine vinegar
¼ level teaspoon cayenne pepper
1 level teaspoon dried oregano

1 Grill the peppers under a moderate heat for 10-12 minutes, turning often, until they are browned all over. Put them in a bowl, cover with a clean damp cloth and set aside. When they are cool enough to handle, pull off their skins, working over a bowl to catch any juice. Remove the seeds and cut the flesh into strips.

2 Meanwhile, put the pork slices between sheets of greaseproof paper and beat them with a rolling pin until they are very thin. Coat the slices lightly with the flour.

3 Heat the oil in a frying pan, and cook the pork slices in it over a moderate heat for 4 minutes on each side. Lay the slices on a plate covered with kitchen paper and set aside.

4 Fry the onion and garlic gently in the same pan for 5 minutes, until softened. Stir in the tomatoes, sultanas, vinegar, cayenne pepper, oregano and any juice from the grilled peppers. Bring to the boil, reduce the heat, cover and cook for 5 minutes, stirring occasionally.

5 Put the pork slices in the sauce, scatter in the pepper strips, cover and heat through for about 5 minutes.

Fresh pasta and a mixed green salad make simple accompaniments for the subtly flavoured pork and its sauce.

DESSERTS

Ices and gâteaux, puddings and pies end a meal with a touch of luxury. When the fat and sugar have been carefully controlled, a moderate portion does no harm in a generally healthy diet. This selection of desserts makes the most of fresh fruits in season for the fibre they contribute.

Apple and raisin crisp

SERVES 6
PREPARATION TIME: 25 minutes
COOKING TIME: 30 minutes
OVEN: Preheat to 150°C (300°F, gas mark 2)

3 medium cooking apples, peeled, cored
and thinly sliced
1 tablespoon lemon juice
3oz (85g) seedless raisins
1½ oz (45g) soft dark brown sugar
1 level teaspoon ground cinnamon

For the topping:
3oz (85g) wholemeal breadcrumbs
1oz (30g) polyunsaturated margarine, melted
1 level tablespoon soft brown sugar
½ level teaspoon ground cinnamon

1   Toss the apples with the lemon juice, then
mix them with the raisins, sugar and cinnamon.

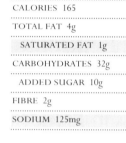

ONE SERVING

CALORIES 165

TOTAL FAT 4g

SATURATED FAT 1g

CARBOHYDRATES 32g

ADDED SUGAR 10g

FIBRE 2g

SODIUM 125mg

Spoon the mixture into an oval ovenproof dish
about 9in (23cm) long.

2   To prepare the topping, spread out the
breadcrumbs on a baking tray and bake in
the heated oven, stirring occasionally, for
15 minutes or until they are dry. Put them in
a small bowl and mix in the margarine, sugar
and the cinnamon. Increase the oven
temperature to 190°C (375°F, gas mark 5).

3   Sprinkle the topping over the apples and
bake in the heated oven for 30 minutes. If the
topping is browning too fast, cover it loosely
with greaseproof or baking paper.

*The acidity of apples and bite of cinnamon are
sweetened by raisins under a top layer of crunchy
wholemeal breadcrumbs and brown sugar.*

Blending a selection of summer berries and yoghurt before, during and after freezing creates a deliciously fresh, smooth, soft ice cream.

Mixed berry ice cream

ONE SERVING	
CALORIES 110	
TOTAL FAT 1g	
SATURATED FAT 0	
CARBOHYDRATES 24g	
ADDED SUGAR 15g	
FIBRE 2g	
SODIUM 45mg	

TIP
To make blending easier, cut the frozen ice cream into cubes before putting it into the food processor.

SERVES 4
PREPARATION TIME: 20 minutes,
plus 4 hours to freeze

*4oz (115g) each fresh raspberries, strawberries
and blackberries, hulled
2oz (60g) caster sugar
2 teaspoons lemon juice
8oz (225g) low-fat natural yoghurt
4 raspberries and pansies, violets or other edible
flowers for decoration*

1 Blend the raspberries, strawberries and blackberries with the sugar in a food processor for 60 seconds to make a smooth purée. Rub the purée into a bowl through a fine nylon sieve to remove the seeds. Mix in the lemon juice and yoghurt. Pour the fruit mixture into a shallow plastic container, cover and freeze for about 1 hour, or until almost solid.

2 Blend the mixture in a food processor again for 1-2 minutes, or until smooth. Freeze for 3 hours or until just frozen. Blend the ice cream again in the food processor until smooth and creamy. Spoon into glasses, top with the raspberries and flowers and serve at once.

You can use frozen fruits in place of fresh. Thaw them before blending to a purée.

Juicy raspberries and crunchy almonds layered with pleasantly tart chocolate-flavoured yoghurt make this a perfect cooling summer treat.

Chocolate berry parfait

ONE SERVING	
CALORIES 205	
TOTAL FAT 10g	
SATURATED FAT 2g	
CARBOHYDRATES 15g	
ADDED SUGAR 5g	
FIBRE 3g	
SODIUM 115mg	

SERVES 4
PREPARATION TIME: 15 minutes,
plus 1-2 hours to chill

12oz (340g) low-fat natural yoghurt
2 level tablespoons cocoa, sifted
1 level tablespoon icing sugar, sifted
8oz (225g) fresh raspberries, or frozen
raspberries, thawed
2oz (60g) blanched almonds, finely chopped
and lightly toasted
4 mint sprigs for decoration

1 Whisk the yoghurt, cocoa and icing sugar until blended.

2 Set aside 4 of the raspberries. Spoon one third of the yoghurt mixture into 4 tall glasses, put half the raspberries on top, and sprinkle on half the toasted almonds.

3 Repeat these layers in each glass, then finish with the remaining yoghurt mixture. Put in the refrigerator to chill for 1-2 hours. Garnish each parfait with a raspberry and sprig of mint just before serving.

You can use strawberries or loganberries in place of raspberries. For a richer mixture, use half and half low-fat and Greek yoghurt, or replace the yoghurt entirely with fromage frais.

Chocolate pudding

SERVES 4
PREPARATION TIME: 5 minutes,
plus 3-4 hours to cool and chill
COOKING TIME: 10 minutes

3 level tablespoons cocoa
1oz (30g) soft light brown sugar
3 level tablespoons cornflour
14fl oz (400ml) skimmed milk
1 teaspoon vanilla extract
Dark chocolate curls for decoration
4 large strawberries, washed and dried

1 Mix the cocoa, sugar and cornflour in a heavy-based saucepan and, using a wire whisk, gradually blend in the milk. Bring the mixture to the boil over a moderate heat, stirring continuously with a wooden spoon. Reduce the heat to low and continue stirring for about 3 minutes, until the cornflour is cooked and the mixture is thickened and smooth.

2 Remove from the heat, stir in the vanilla extract and pour into 4 small individual dishes. Cover with wetted greaseproof paper and when they are cool, put them, still covered, in the refrigerator to chill for about 3 hours. Just before serving, decorate each pudding with chocolate curls and a strawberry.

You can use finely grated orange rind instead of, or in addition to, the vanilla extract.

ONE SERVING

CALORIES 125

TOTAL FAT 2g

SATURATED FAT 1g

CARBOHYDRATES 23g

ADDED SUGAR 8g

FIBRE 1g

SODIUM 135mg

TIP
To make chocolate curls, spread 2-3 squares of melted dark chocolate thinly on a clean marble slab or laminated plastic surface. As soon as the chocolate is dry to the touch, push a knife blade against it to lift it in curls.

Luscious strawberries give these little pots of smooth dark chocolate a fresh finish in a luxury dessert that is surprisingly low in calories and simplicity itself to prepare.

Orange and strawberry flan

SERVES 6
PREPARATION TIME: 25 minutes,
plus 30 minutes to cool
COOKING TIME: 20 minutes
OVEN: Preheat to 200°C (400°F, gas mark 6)

½ teaspoon corn oil
2 eggs, size 2
1½ oz (45g) caster sugar
2oz (60g) plain flour
6oz (175g) curd cheese
Finely grated rind and juice of 1 orange
4oz (115g) strawberries, washed, dried well
and halved
2 oranges, peel and white pith removed, cut
into thin slices

1 Lightly rub the oil over a nonstick sponge
flan tin 8½ in (21cm) in diameter, and line the
base with nonstick baking paper.

2 Whisk the eggs and caster sugar in a bowl,
using an electric or a rotary hand whisk.
Continue until the mixture is very fluffy and
so thick that a ribbon of the mixture trailed
onto it from the whisk stays on the surface.

3 Sift the flour lightly over the egg mixture,
and fold in carefully with a large metal spoon.
Pour into the flan tin and spread evenly to the
edges. Bake in the centre of the heated oven for
about 20 minutes, or until well risen, lightly
browned and springy to the touch.

4 Gently ease the sponge from the edges of
the tin with a palette knife and turn out onto a
wire rack to cool for 30 minutes. Remove the
baking paper.

5 Mix the curd cheese with the orange rind
and juice until smooth.

6 Place the flan case flat side down and fill the
central hollow with the curd cheese mixture,
spreading it evenly. Decorate the top with the
strawberry halves and orange slices.

ONE SERVING

CALORIES 170

TOTAL FAT 6g

SATURATED FAT 3g

CARBOHYDRATES 22g

ADDED SUGAR 8g

FIBRE 1g

SODIUM 145mg

*A smooth but lively orange-curd filling is sandwiched
between a light and golden sponge base and a
fragrant pairing of strawberry halves and orange
slices, achieving a perfect balance between the sweet
and the tart in this fresh-fruit flan.*

Peach and almond strudel

SERVES 6
PREPARATION TIME: 30 minutes
COOKING TIME: 45 minutes
OVEN: Preheat to 200°C (400°F, gas mark 6)

ONE SERVING

CALORIES 215

TOTAL FAT 9g

SATURATED FAT 1g

CARBOHYDRATES 29g

ADDED SUGAR 3g

FIBRE 3g

SODIUM 180mg

1½ oz (45g) ground almonds
1 level tablespoon caster sugar
1 level teaspoon ground mixed spice
Finely grated rind of 1 lemon
1½ oz (45g) wholemeal breadcrumbs
6oz (175g) filo pastry sheets
1oz (30g) polyunsaturated margarine, melted
4 large ripe peaches, skinned, stoned and sliced

TIP
*If the peach skins
will not pull off
easily, put the fruit
in a heatproof bowl,
pour boiling water
over them, leave for
1 minute then rinse
with cold water.
The skin will come
away easily.*

1   Mix the almonds, sugar, spice and lemon rind with 1oz (30g) of the breadcrumbs.

2   On a large clean teacloth, lay half the sheets of pastry, trimmed as necessary and with edges overlapping, to form a rectangle about 20×16in (51×40cm). Arrange the rectangle so that one of its long sides is nearest to you. Brush lightly with melted margarine. Arrange a second layer of pastry sheets on top in the same way and brush with a little more margarine.

3   Spread the ground almond mixture in a 4in (10cm) strip along the side nearest to you, setting it in 2in (50mm) from the edge. Arrange the peach slices on top of the mixture.

4   Fold the two short sides in by 1in (25mm), and fold the clear 2in (50mm) strip of pastry over the peaches. Lift the edge of the teacloth nearest to you so that the strudel begins to roll away from you. Keep lifting until the strudel is completely rolled. Carefully lay the strudel, seam side down, on a nonstick baking sheet.

5   Brush the remaining margarine over the strudel and sprinkle with the remaining breadcrumbs. Bake in the heated oven for about 45 minutes, or until the pastry is golden brown and crisp. Serve the strudel warm.

When fresh peaches are unavailable use 1¾ lb (800g) of unsweetened tinned peach halves, drained, dried with kitchen paper and sliced. For a special occasion, sift 1 level teaspoon of icing sugar over the strudel and put a teaspoon of Greek yoghurt beside each serving.

Melting, spiced almond paste and fresh peach slices in a wafer-thin wrapping create this tempting variation of the Viennese apple strudel.

Gooseberry pancakes

ONE SERVING	
CALORIES	245
TOTAL FAT	5g
SATURATED FAT	2g
CARBOHYDRATES	43g
ADDED SUGAR	11g
FIBRE	4g
SODIUM	65mg

SERVES 4
PREPARATION TIME: *20 minutes*
COOKING TIME: *35 minutes*
OVEN: *Preheat to 190°C (375°F, gas mark 5)*

Finely grated rind and juice of ¹/₂ orange
1oz (30g) soft light brown sugar
1lb (450g) ripe dessert gooseberries, topped and tailed
4oz (115g) plain wholemeal flour

1 egg, size 2, beaten
¹/₂ pint (285ml) semi-skimmed milk
2 teaspoons corn oil
Squares of greaseproof paper for stacking
1 level tablespoon demerara sugar

1 Gently heat the orange rind and juice with the light brown sugar in a saucepan, stirring to dissolve the sugar. Put in the gooseberries and simmer for about 10 minutes, stirring occasionally, until they are soft and the juice is slightly thickened. Leave to cool.

2 Put the flour in a mixing bowl, make a well in the centre and pour in the egg and half the milk. Stir well with a wooden spoon until the ingredients are combined, then beat until smooth. Stir in the remaining milk and pour the batter into a measuring jug.

3 Smear a little oil over the base of a nonstick frying pan 6in (15cm) in diameter. Heat it over a moderate heat until it gives off a slight haze. Pour one-eighth of the batter into the pan and quickly tilt the pan until the base is coated thinly. Cook until the top of the batter is set and the underside golden brown. Turn or toss the pancake over and cook the other side. Slide out onto a plate. Make seven more pancakes in the same way and put greaseproof paper between them as you stack them on the plate.

4 Lay the pancakes with the side cooked first down on the work surface. Divide the filling between the pancakes and spread evenly. Fold each one in half, then in half again to make a fan shape and overlap the fans in an ovenproof dish. Sprinkle the demerara sugar over the top.

5 Place in the heated oven for 15 minutes, until heated through and crisp round the edges. Serve immediately.

When you cannot get dessert gooseberries, use a cooking variety, but you might need to add more sugar. You can make the pancakes a day ahead, let them cool and keep them in the refrigerator in a polythene bag.

Dessert gooseberries with their full flavour and slightly acid tang make a refreshing filling for fans of pancakes with a crisp, sweet demerara topping.

A generous dash of orange liqueur accentuates the warm citrus flavour of this light, frothy soufflé, which is particularly low in calories yet brings a touch of luxury to the end of a meal.

ONE SERVING	
CALORIES 80	
TOTAL FAT 1g	
SATURATED FAT 0	
CARBOHYDRATES 15g	
ADDED SUGAR 10g	
FIBRE 0	
SODIUM 65mg	

Orange soufflé

SERVES 6
PREPARATION TIME: 20 minutes, plus 1 hour to cool
COOKING TIME: 30 minutes
OVEN: Preheat to 180°C (350°F, gas mark 4)

2oz (60g) granulated sugar
1½ level tablespoons cornflour
4fl oz (115ml) skimmed milk
1 egg, separated, plus 3 egg whites, size 2
2 tablespoons orange liqueur
Finely grated rind of 2 oranges
½ teaspoon vanilla extract

1 Mix the sugar and cornflour in a saucepan, then stir in the milk little by little. Bring to the boil over a moderate heat, stirring continuously. Reduce the heat to low and simmer, stirring, for 30 seconds.

2 Remove from the heat and cool slightly. Beat in the egg yolk, orange liqueur, orange rind and vanilla extract. Pour the custard into a bowl and lay a disc of wetted nonstick baking paper directly on it to prevent a skin from forming on top. Leave the custard for about 1 hour to cool to room temperature.

3 Whisk the egg whites until they hold soft peaks. Fold 1 tablespoon of the egg white into the orange mixture to lighten it, then gently fold in the rest of the egg white. Spoon the mixture into a deep soufflé dish 7in (18cm) in diameter. Bake in the heated oven for about 30 minutes, or until the soufflé is well risen and lightly browned on top. Serve immediately.

Use Seville oranges when they are in season, for a particularly zesty soufflé.

Plum cobbler

ONE SERVING	
CALORIES	280
TOTAL FAT	8g
SATURATED FAT	1g
CARBOHYDRATES	48g
ADDED SUGAR	8g
FIBRE	4g
SODIUM	245mg

SERVES 6
PREPARATION TIME: 30 minutes
COOKING TIME: 45 minutes
OVEN: Preheat to 200°C (400°F, gas mark 6)

1½ lb (680g) ripe Victoria plums or Spanish
dessert plums, halved and stoned
1½ oz (45g) soft light brown sugar
1oz (30g) ground almonds
6 tablespoons water

For the topping:
6oz (175g) self-raising flour
2oz (60g) plain wholemeal flour
1 level teaspoon baking powder
1oz (30g) polyunsaturated margarine
1 egg, size 2, lightly beaten
7 tablespoons skimmed milk
1 teaspoon caster sugar

Mellow dessert plums, their juice thickened by ground almonds, are baked beneath thick rounds of low-fat scone pastry in this warming family pudding for autumn days.

1 Mix the plums with the brown sugar, ground almonds and water. Spread the mixture in an ovenproof dish 8in (20cm) in diameter.

2 To make the topping, combine the flours and baking powder in a bowl, and rub in the margarine. Pour in the egg and 6 tablespoons of the milk, and mix to form a soft dough. Knead to an even texture on a lightly floured surface.

3 Roll out the dough on a lightly floured surface to ½ in (13mm) thick. Use a fluted 2½ in (65mm) cutter to cut rounds from the dough. Knead and roll the trimmings and cut out more rounds to make 12 in all. Lay them,

slightly overlapping, in a circle round the dish and brush with the remaining milk.

4 Bake in the heated oven for 45 minutes, or until the rounds are golden and the plums soft. Cover with greaseproof paper after 30 minutes so the top does not brown too much. Sprinkle the cobbler with the caster sugar and serve hot.

If you like, you can add 1 teaspoon of vanilla extract to the dough. A spoonful of Greek yoghurt on each serving would add a touch of luxury. If you cannot get ripe Victoria or Spanish dessert plums you can use a cooking variety, but you might have to add more sugar.